3/2/8

ANNE OF BRITTANY.
Age about 15.

A TWICE CROWNED QUEEN

ANNE OF BRITTANY

BY

CONSTANCE, COUNTESS DE LA WARR

LONDON
EVELEIGH NASH
1906

INTRODUCTION

———◆———

No one who travels either in Brittany or Touraine can fail to be impressed by the great personality of Anne of Brittany, with which these two Provinces are impregnated. Whether you go to the large towns or small villages, you will find remains testifying to her life within them, either in the form of castles, such as Blois, Amboise, Loches, where she lived in great splendour, or of houses on a smaller scale at Dinan, Morlaix, Vannes, and Nantes, or, yet again of the many fine churches and convents which she erected and endowed.

She truly loved her Brittany, and greatly desired it to retain its position as an independent State, which it had more or less succeeded in doing until her own accession to its sovereignty on the death of her father, Duke

Introduction

Francis II., in 1488. It had, however, all along been a severe struggle for the Bretons to prevent their Duchy from falling into the hands, either of France or England, — the former country, especially, had ever looked upon it with a greedy eye, and had made many a raid upon the coveted land, — but though beaten on several occasions, they had again and again freed themselves from their invaders.

Anne, being only twelve years old at the death of her father, Charles VIII. of France felt he could not lose so good an opportunity of adding another jewel to the French crown, and decided to try the arts of love instead of those of war. He proclaimed himself the rightful guardian of the young Duchess, saying that it was his duty and that of France to watch over her. Anne in vain protested; but when, later on, he offered her his heart and crown, promising the young girl that she should remain sole ruler of her beloved country, and that its union with France would be but a nominal transaction, one cannot wonder that this assurance, and the triumph

Introduction

and honour of having the French king at her feet, overcame her objections, and led her to accept Charles' proposal, although she had been affianced, before her father's death, to Maximilian of Austria, as will be seen in the following history.

Brittany, in truth, tired out with all the fighting and feuds she was ever engaged in, accepted the alliance with more or less good grace, feeling also that so small a State could not long withstand the growing power of France. From this time Brittany virtually became a French province, though to the present day the inhabitants still retain their individual and independent spirit, and are honest, brave, religious, and simple. The national costume is still worn, and in many ways the people are quite a distinct type from the rest of France. It is really quite refreshing in these days to find a race which is not the counterpart of its neighbours, and mix with people whose ideas remain fresh and simple; and I am sure that no one would ever regret devoting time and study to this lovely country and its inhabitants.

Introduction

Anne's connection with Touraine began after her marriage with Charles VIII., and her history becomes still more interwoven with that part of France when she was the wife of Louis XII., so those who have time should visit the beautiful castles there connected with the life of the twice crowned Queen of France.

CONTENTS

ix

Contents

x

WORKS CONSULTED

Vie de la Reine Anne de Bretagne .	LE ROUX DE LINCY.
Louis XII. et Anne de Bretagne .	LACROIX.
Dames Illustres . . .	BRANTÔME.
Les Femmes de la Renaissance .	R. DE MAULDE LA CLAVIÈRE.
Chroniques de Louis XII. . .	JEAN D'AUTON.
Louis XII.	ZELLER.
Women and Men of the French Renaissance	EDITH SICHEL.
Ferdinand and Isabella . .	PRESCOTT.
Histoire de Charles VIII., 1864 .	GODEFROI.
Lettres du Roy Louis XII., 1712 .	
Memoirs of the Kings of France .	WRAXALL.
Isabella d'Este . . .	MRS. ADY.
Dukes and Poets in Ferrara .	EDMUND G. GARDNER, M.A.

A TWICE CROWNED QUEEN

＋

CHAPTER I

Birth of Anne of Brittany—Her Education—The Suitors for
  her Hand—Her Marriage by Proxy with Maximilian
  of Austria, King of the Romans—Siege of Rennes by
  Charles VIII., King of France—Capture of this Town by
  the French—Negotiations for the Marriage of Anne of
  Brittany with Charles VIII.

BRITTANY, so often a prey to wars within and
without,—within, owing to her civil discords, and
without, arising from the rapacity of her neighbours,—had from the middle of the fifteenth
century enjoyed a comparative period of peace,
and attained, under the rule of her sovereign,
Duke Francis II., the height of her prosperity.

Duke Francis was a sovereign in advance
of his times ; he loved literature, painting, and
sculpture, founded schools and universities,

A   I

A Twice Crowned Queen

encouraged commerce, and caused artists and
tapestry-workers from Flanders to settle in his
capital, Nantes, where their tapestries soon
became famous. So prosperous did his subjects become during his reign, that it is said,
even the peasants ate out of silver vessels,
while more often than not the inhabitants of
the ports slept on silver couches.* Unfortunately, the moral character of the Duke did
not rise to the height of his intellect, and led
to the non-continuance of this happy state of
things.

He was twice married, first to his cousin,
Marguerite of Brittany, by whom he had a
son, called the Comte de Montfort, who died
soon after his birth, 25th August 1465. This
unhappy wife, neglected for his mistress,
Antoinette de Maignelais, died of consump-
tion in 1469.

In 1471, Francis married Marguerite, sister
of the Comte de Foix, who in due course
gave him two children, Anne, born in the
Castle of Nantes at 6.30 a.m. on 25th January
1476, and Isabeau, born a few years later.

* Cimber, *Archives Curieuses de l'Histoire de France.*

2

A Twice Crowned Queen

Both these births were a source of severe disappointment to Francis, who greatly desired a son, and they were looked upon by his people as a punishment from God for his infidelity as a husband. His mistress died in 1475, and although we do not hear of another taking her place, he surrounded himself with unworthy favourites, male and female. Among them was a man of bourgeois birth, Pierre Landais, of Vitré, the son of a merchant in cloth and silk. These cloth merchants held an important place in the Corporation of the town, and their chiefs often obtained the first rank of nobility. The Court often came to Vitré, and it was on one of these occasions that Pierre attracted the attention of Duke Francis, who took him into his service as valet. A man of great shrewdness and re-markable talent, he lost no time in ingratiating himself with his master, studied his tastes, pandered to his inclinations, and missed no opportunity of gratifying them. He quickly grew in favour, and one post after another was conferred upon him, until, to the amaze-ment and disgust of the nobles, he was appointed Treasurer-General, in which capacity he was able to supply the Duke's mistress with money for her needs. The pride and arrogance he displayed in his new office made him universally hated; there was no limit to his power; he controlled the revenue, dictated to foreign princes, and when it came in the way of his ambition, had no scruple in setting aside his sovereign's will. At last he became Prime Minister, and completely ruled his master. His extravagance increased daily, and the once prosperous Brittany became a prey to the rapacity of those who played into the hands of this dreaded favourite. At last, exasperated by his cruelties and crimes, the Bretons, who could get no redress from their Duke, took the law into their own hands, surrounded the palace, and with threats and cries demanded that Landais should be given up to them. The Duke sent the Comte de Foix to appease them, but he returned in haste exclaiming—

"I would rather be prince over a million wild boars than over such people as your Bretons; you will certainly have to give up

your treasurer, or we shall all be mur-
dered." *

The Duke, finding himself powerless, gave
up his favourite, who was at once tried, condemned, and executed.

Returning to the birth of Anne, we find
that the Demoiselle de la Vire was sent for
from Rennes to be the infant's nurse; but
she was not approved of by the doctors, who
chose the wife of Jean Eon, also of Rennes,
to take her place. Her education was entrusted to the care of one of the greatest
ladies of the Duchy, Françoise de Dinan, of
the House of d'Albret, Dame de Château-
briand and Laval. The House of Laval had
made alliances with many crowned heads, and
in 1451, at the Assembly of the Estates of
the Province, claimed precedence over that of
Rohan. Françoise de Dinan proved herself
worthy both of her high lineage and of the
precious charge committed to her care. She
watched over the young Duchess with tender-
ness, endeavoured to make her education as
complete as possible in every branch, and

* Lobineau, *Histoire de Bretagne.*

A Twice Crowned Queen

trained her mind in all that was good and noble.

Anne was a child of quick apprehension and intelligent mind; she was instructed in Greek and Latin, but never became a scholar; later in life, "though she could not read Latin, she liked nothing better than to talk about Livy and to have learned works dedicated to her." * Before she was nine years old, however, she was looked upon as a most accomplished Princess, and in 1485, when Louis d'Orleans came to Brittany, he was astonished at her charms and the precocity of her mind. The attention this Prince then showed her gave rise to the ridiculous report that he was seriously in love with her; but no one on reflection could give credence to such an idea, or suppose that he had other feelings than those which a quick, pretty, and clever child would inspire. Besides, this Prince was already married, and he could not then have found any pretext for a separation. His frequent journeys to the Court of Brittany may have given rise to the report, which

* Edith Sichel, *Women and Men of the French Renaissance.*

Louis indeed found it necessary to contradict, and he publicly declared that his visits to the Duke were merely to help and advise him in many points connected with the defence of his Duchy, and not for the purpose of proposing marriage with either of his daughters.* When twelve years old, Anne wrote with her own hand, and sent to Maximilian, King of the Romans, a narrative of the events which had just taken place in Brittany, with a description of the battle of Saint-Aubin-le-Cormier.

In her ninth year she lost her beloved mother, Marguerite de Foix, whose saintly and gentle spirit slipped away from her sad life, after a short illness, in 1485. Deprived as she had been of her husband's love, she had given all her affection to her young daughters, whose grief at their mother's loss was unbounded. Beyond her beauty and accomplishments, and the purity of her life, little is known of her. "Laissant après soy la réputation d'avoir été l'une des plus belles princesses de son temps et autant accomplie en bonne mœurs qu'aucune autre de son âge," as

* *Archives de Nantes.*

d'Argentré says. She rests, with her faithless husband and his first wife, in the beautiful tomb erected by her daughter Anne in Nantes Cathedral.

Francis II. with all his faults was not a bad father, and gave his daughters as much affection as he was capable of after their mother's death, and they accompanied him in his journeys to his various castles and fortresses. So unsettled was the state of Brittany in the last years of his life, that he had to move secretly from place to place for safety, and at a time when he was besieged in Nantes by the French army he quitted his apartments in the castle for a more secure dwelling in the town, and his daughters were taken to the Hôtel de la Bouvadière.

No doubt this exciting and wandering life had great charms for the young girls after the quiet life they had led with their mother, and it must have been a grief to them when, in October 1488, three years after their mother's death, Duke Francis died at Coiron, on the Loire, where, with his two daughters and Court, he had been obliged to retire on account of the plague which was raging at Nantes. Grief at the loss of the battle of Saint Aubin is said to have caused his death ; but, doubtless, his wild and intemperate life had much to do with it.

Though not respected by his people, Francis, by his good-nature and handsome bearing, had gained their affection to a certain degree, and his liberality to those he liked made his loss mourned by many.

It was a trying position for Anne, who was only twelve years old, to be left mistress of one of the oldest duchies in Europe ; and what a burden of responsibility to fall on such young shoulders !

In his will, Duke Francis appointed the Maréchal de Rieux and the Comte de Comminges to be guardians to his two daughters, recommending them both not to act without the advice and approval of the Comte de Dunois ; and he desired that Madame de Laval should still remain with the Princesses as their governess, but he made no mention of the marriage of Anne or of her sister.

Directly after their father's death, they

were taken from Coiron to Guérande, which was considered a safer place for them in such unsettled times.

The Breton nobles had taken the oath of allegiance to Anne while her father was still alive, and among them was François, Baron d'Avaugour, her natural brother, son of Antoinette de Maignelais, for whom Anne had much affection.

She was at once proclaimed the Duke's successor, and no time was lost in sending an embassy to Charles VIII. to announce the event, he, in return, despatching a special messenger to condole with and congratulate the young Duchess, assuring her that it was his intention to keep the treaty of peace, signed a short time after the battle of Saint Aubin. By this treaty, Francis not only gave up to Charles the towns of Fougères, Dinan, Saint Aubin and Saint Malo, but also recognised this Prince's rights to the Duchy of Brittany, and agreed not to marry his daughters without Charles' consent.

Charles VIII. now begged Anne to agree to three propositions, (1) that being nearly related to her, he should be the guardian of herself and her sister, and should have entire charge of their lands and lordships during their minority; (2) that as there were disputes with regard to their respective rights to the Duchy, the titles on each side should be produced, in order that arbitrators should be appointed immediately to decide the question; (3) that all strangers should leave the country, according to the treaty.

Anne's reply to these propositions was that she had no intention of infringing the articles of the treaty, and that she had already convoked the Estates of Brittany to ratify it.

Anne's position was clearly one of great difficulty and danger; the extravagance of Landais and the expense of the wars had exhausted the Treasury; her Ministers were all of different opinions, each thinking only of his own interests and not of those of the orphan ruler of thirteen; the plague was still raging in many parts of the Duchy, and a French army was ready at any moment to invade her already desolate country.

Truly, many a young girl would have broken

11

down under such a strain; not so Anne, all her Breton energy and courage came out, and the strong will and character she was so noted for during her whole life showed itself in her reply to her Ministers at the first meeting of the Estates. They found they had no weak girl to deal with, but a resolute woman whose will refused to yield to intimidation. She stated clearly and decidedly what she intended to do.

Her marriage, and the man she would select as worthy of her hand, was now the burning question, for the future and independence of Brittany hung on the decision. Since 1480, Francis II. had tried to arrange this important business; the hand of Anne, or failing her, that of her sister, had been promised to the eldest son of Edward IV. King of England, but in 1483 the poor young prince was assassinated by his uncle, Richard III.

Then negotiations were opened for an alliance with Maximilian, Duke of Austria, who for a year had been a widower; his young wife, Mary of Burgundy, had died suddenly, leaving him with two children, a son and a daughter. The latter, though only three years old, was betrothed to Charles, then Dauphin, and sent to the French Court to be brought up. Of all the foreign alliances this one seemed the most advantageous, though it did not give any guarantee for the independence and maintenance of Brittany's nationality. The Bretons themselves thought the best means for this end would have been to marry the young Duchess to one of their own nobles, chosen from those who already had pretensions to the ducal crown. These were three in number, Jean de Châlons Prince of Orange, son of Duke Francis II.'s sister; Jean Vicomte de Rohan, married to Marie, daughter of Duke Francis I., who claimed to be the direct descendant of Conan Mériadec, first King of Brittany; Alain Seigneur d'Albret, married to a great-granddaughter of Jeanne la Boiteuse, brother of the Dame de Laval, the young Duchess's governess. When Francis II. died, the last alone of these three suitors was a widower, and owing to the influence of his sister, he had gained the suffrages of those Bretons who desired to maintain the independence of their country.

A Twice Crowned Queen

He himself was a strange suitor to propose for the hand of the poor little Princess. He was more than forty-five; his spotted face, harsh voice, fierce expression, and still fiercer temper were not likely to attract a girl of thirteen, and the contemporary, Jaligny, who gives us this portrait, adds, "la fille n'en avait cure."

The Vicomte de Rohan's hopes were centred in a plan to marry his eldest son to Anne, and his second son to Isabeau, as soon as they should be of marriageable age; but he forgot, in his presumption, that for many years he had fought in the French army, and Bretons, faithful to their country, looked upon him as an enemy.

Jean de Châlons, taken prisoner at the battle of Saint Aubin, had regained his liberty in February 1488, and his first step on his return to Nantes was to try to prevent the savage d'Albret from succeeding in his attempts to marry the young Duchess. He therefore favoured the suit of Maximilian of Austria, allowed two thousand Spaniards, sent by King Ferdinand, to enter Brittany, and signed a document in which he bound himself not to negotiate for the marriage of the Duchess Anne without the advice and consent of this powerful monarch. This agreement was signed at Rennes " on the seventh day of the month of April 1489, before Easter." *

In 1490, having attained her fourteenth year, the lords of her Council advised Anne to make this alliance with Maximilian. Of an age to understand the importance of such an act, she accepted the union with the King of the Romans, flattered at the idea of being a Queen, and cherishing the hope of one day wearing the Imperial crown. This put an end to the importunities of the Dame de Laval, who urged her every day, for the love of her country, to marry the fierce Alain d'Albret, whose look alone made her shudder.

The negotiations for her marriage, by proxy, to the King of the Romans were made with the utmost secrecy in March 1490, lest Charles should be informed and put his veto upon it ; for it was in direct violation of the treaty made with him, that, as guardian of the Duchess, no marriage should be arranged without his consent.

* MS. British Museum.

A Twice Crowned Queen

Maximilian entrusted the Comte de Nassau, the Seigneur de Polhain, his maréchal, Jacques de Coudebault, his secretary, and Louppain, his steward, with the mission to Brittany, in order to arrange the affair completely, and even to proceed with the ceremony of betrothal. A few days after—the exact day has never been known —this ceremony took place according to German custom, and being a curious one may be of interest. The young Duchess was put to bed, and the handsome Polhain, Maximilian's favourite, placed his leg, naked up to the knee, in the nuptial couch, in presence, let it be understood, of three other envoys, and of Françoise de Dinan and several members of the household.*

Maximilian seems to have made a fatal error in not coming to plead his own cause with the young Duchess, when probably a real marriage would have taken place instead of the betrothal by proxy, which, though valid in point of law, could by influence be made null.

So important an act could not long remain secret, and the Chancellor of Brittany,

* *Chroniques de Jean Molinet.*

Montauban, was one of the first to divulge it, making his mistress, Anne, sign herself Queen of the Romans in many public deeds. The French were greatly incensed when the details became known, the Bretons resented the privacy of the whole affair, and together they turned into ridicule the ceremony of betrothal, laughing at customs so different from their own.

Alain d'Albret burst into a violent temper and bitter complaints, avowing publicly that Duke Francis had promised him his daughter's hand, and that Anne had accepted him as a husband. He failed to mention that the young Princess had but done it on compulsion, when only ten years old, in obedience to her father's wishes; and to show that she had no intention of any such alliance, Anne, after Francis II.'s death, sent a protest to the Ecclesiastical Court, saying, that if, when she was only ten years of age, any promise of marriage had been drawn from her, she now entirely repudiated it.*

D'Albret, furious at being foiled in his designs, swiftly took his revenge. The Gascon

* *Archives de Bretagne.*

bands which he commanded were in possession of the citadel of Nantes, and kept the town in awe. He made it known to the chiefs of the French army that he was willing to treat with them; and when Charles VIII., after being assured of the truth of the information concerning the violated treaty, invested Nantes, the town was given up, almost without a struggle, by Alain d'Albret, who abandoned all his rights to the Duchy of Brittany on condition of receiving a pension of £25,000. He still clung, however, to the hope of a marriage with Anne, knowing that France did not acknowledge the validity of the union with Maximilian, and actually had the following clause inserted in the agreement with Charles: "that it should please the King to give the hand of Madame Anne of Brittany in marriage to the said Seigneur d'Albret, or his son, and to favour them in the matter, and by all fair means to bring the said marriage about." *

Charles, though he may have seemed to agree to d'Albret's desires, had far different aims in view, and early in the year 1491, accompanied

* *Actes de Bretagne.*

CHARLES VIII.

by the Comte de Dunois, Louis duc d'Orleans,
and the Dame de Beaujeu, entered Brittany to
join his army there. He held his Court at
Nantes, and tried in every way to ingratiate
himself with the Bretons. Bribes were given
and received by the heads of the rival factions
which had rent Brittany in pieces since the
death of Duke Francis. Louis XI. had gained
over to his interests many important Breton
nobles, and Anne de Beaujeu had carried on
her father's work so successfully, that very
few of Anne's subjects remained faithful
to her.

Anne herself, at the head of a little army
under the command of the Maréchal de Rieux,
her guardian, tried vainly to struggle against the
French invasion. She was in grave distress
for money, so much so that the Maréchal had
caused a rough piece of money, called "black
money," to be issued. This was of little value in
itself, being made of leather with a small piece
of silver in the centre.*

---

* This sort of money was common in France when King Jean
le Bon was a captive in England, after the battle of Poitiers.
"Because there was no money, they made a very small coin in

A Twice Crowned Queen

Besides this, he had pledged Anne's jewels, flagons, bonbonnières, and even the shrines in which the Host was placed, the whole weighing little over five hundred silver marks.

The following document is interesting on account of the minute description of the objects mentioned above :—

"RENNES, *9th August* 1460.

"Letters patent of the Duchess Anne, by which, on representations made to her by her well-beloved and leal cousin, the Comtesse de Laval and by her well-beloved and leal cousin, the Seigneur de Rieux, her lieutenant-general and Maréchal of Brittany, that since for four years past the French under arms had invaded her States, where they had committed an infinitude of outrages, burnt and pillaged churches, taken towns and fortresses, and killed a great number of her subjects ; and that during this time differences having arisen between some of her near relations, servitors and subjects, and that on account of these things, having wished to retire with her very dear and much loved

silver, and attached it to a piece of leather in order that it should not be lost, and also be more convenient for handling" (Godefroi et Langlet du Fresnoy).

sister, Isabeau of Brittany, to her town of
Nantes, they refused to let her enter together
with the large number of people who accompanied her, and she retired to her town of
Rennes, the said French, profiting by the mis-
understanding existing between the above-
mentioned relations and servitors of the said
Duchess, endeavoured to conquer the towns
of Nantes, Redon, Guerrande and others ; and
having for this purpose tried to pass the river
Villaigne, the Sire de Rieux together with the
troops of the Sire d'Albret prevented them,
so that they were obliged to retire towards
Lower Brittany, where they were in possession
of nearly all the towns, but the said Sire de
Rieux pursued them, so that, with the help
the King of England sent to the said Duchess,
he reconquered nearly all the towns they had
taken, notably that of Coucy ; and afterwards
laid siege to the Castle of Brest, where he
remained for the space of three months, on
account of which things he was put to immense
expense, to defray which the said Maréchal
caused money to be issued, to wit, large pieces
of two sous six farthings, and other black
money of baser alloy.—Item, the said Maréchal
having taken several gold and silver jewels
which the said Duchess had in the town of

Nantes, to wit; two silver-gilt flagons in Venetian work, with two handles, ornamented with enamels set in gold, the said enamels of many figures, and the said enamel of pure red, and with many figures on the covers of the said flagons; those two flagons weighing 207 marcs, 4 onces, 7 gros.—Item, two large bonbonnières, of Milan workmanship, all silver-gilt ornamented with enamels, set in gold, enamelled in pure red, with many kinds of figures, at the foot of which bonbonnières, were four figures of angels with instruments; and on the bowls much of like fashion, their covers enamelled within and without; and of like enamel as are the said bonbonnières one figure at the top, holding in one hand a shield sown with ermines, and in the other a halberd; these bonbonnières and their covers weighing 239 marcs of silver-gilt . . . the whole weighing 500 marcs, 4 onces, 7 gros silver-gilt, all which things the said Duchess approves and ratifies and, moreover, forgets and forgives all that took place at the siege of Guerrande by the soldiers then in the town of Nantes, and by many of the citizens of the said town of Nantes, when her well-loved and leal councillor and chamberlain, Philippe de Montauban, knight and chancellor, was in command for the Duchess;

as also before the Castle of Machecoul, where, it was said, there were around the said places people who robbed the passers-by; wishes that all which her cousin, the Maréchal de Rieux, has done in taking or levying money from her subjects or from the revenue of her domain, be granted and approved by the Councillors of her Exchequer at Rennes, just as though it were herself who had done it, etc.

"Given in her town of Rennes, 9th August 1490.

"Anne.

"By command of the Duchess,
     G. de Forestz,
(Ms. 'Blancs Manteaux,' Paris)."

Anne, as the above document states, being refused admittance at the gates of Nantes, retired with her sister Isabeau to Rennes, while her troops under the Maréchal de Rieux repulsed the French, resisting them desperately at Brest, St. Malo, and many other towns, so that the conquest of the Duchy was not as rapid as it is generally supposed. With her in Rennes were the Prince of Orange, her uncle, the Maréchal de Polhain, and a few faithful barons. Her army consisted of

14,000 men, chiefly composed of English, German, and Spanish archers sent by the King of the Romans to defend her; but how could this mixed body of troops hold out against the French King who was steadily and surely gaining ground all over Brittany, and daily obtaining more and more influence over the people! About the time of the Feast of All Saints, 1491, the town of Rennes was besieged with such mighty engines and so much artillery, that 3000 horses would not have been enough to draw them. A chivalrous incident, illustrative of the manners of the times, took place during the siege, and is thus related by the chronicler, Jean de Molinet:

"The Bastard de Foix, mounted like St. George, approached the walls of the town and asked if any knight would break a lance with him, in honour of the ladies. A Breton lord armed *cap à pie* hastened to present himself. The lists were set up in the trenches of the town, where the young Duchess had scaffolding erected, and to which, attended by a goodly company, she repaired to view the combat. After having broken four or five lances they used their swords and fought very well, and there was no death on either side. This spectacle finished," says Molinet, "the Queen ordered hippocras and spices to be given to the French, and then all retired."

The day after this joust was thought by the besieged an opportune moment to make a sortie against the enemy, and they directed all their efforts against that part of the army commanded by a valiant knight, François d'Ursé. The Germans, coming up first, made a great slaughter, and, thinking they had gained a complete victory, began to plunder and busy themselves with the prisoners; but those in the French camp hastened to the assistance of their comrades, and repulsed the would-be conquerors so violently, that they were obliged to leave their booty and retreat to the town with great precipitation. From that day Charles carried on the siege with greater vigour than ever, and the resources of the town daily became less, food and money grew scarce, and the German and English mercenaries began to mutiny; the former, beating their big drums as a signal to retire, told

the Duchess' officers that they wished to be
paid a week in advance, and the English
followed their example. Poor Anne, who
throughout these trying times had shown a
courage far beyond her years, besides sharing
in all the sufferings and privations of the
besieged, had now to decide whether or not
to accept an offer made by Charles that she
should receive 100,000 crowns a year, provided she gave up the government of Brittany,
and selected as a dwelling any place she liked
except the towns of Rennes and Nantes; he
also offered for her choice three husbands,
Louis de Luxembourg, the Duc de Nemours,
and the Comte d'Angoulême. Anne made no
reply to the offer of money, but with regard
to the matrimonial proposal, replied, that she
was already married to the King of the
Romans, and that, even if he refused to have
her she would never marry anyone else, and
that if he died she would only accept a king
or the son of a king for a husband.

Neither Anne nor any of those round her
felt inclined to accept these hard conditions,
dictated by a merciless conqueror, who, seeing

that the resolution of the young Duchess was not to be shaken, tried other means. He began by offering arrears of pay to the foreign troops who composed the garrison at Rennes on condition that they should immediately depart. The mercenaries accepted the offer, and retired to the town of Montfort, four leagues from Nantes, where they received the three months' pay due to them. After having proclaimed a general amnesty, Charles sent his vanguard, under the command of the Dukes of Orleans and Bourbon, to take possession of the town. Charles then made a new proposition to the Duchess, that of renouncing for ever the Duchy of Brittany on condition of receiving £100,000 a year; she could then join the King of the Romans, whom she looked upon as her husband.

Anne's councillors addressed to the King a memorial full of remonstrances,* but Charles was as stubborn as the Duchess, and partly by menaces and still more by promises, gained over these worthies, and persuaded them to influence the mind of their young mistress,

* *Archives de Nantes.*

so that she should overcome the repugnance she felt towards him. Jean de Châlons, the Maréchal de Rieux, and Françoise de Dinan succeeded in their efforts so far, that Anne began to waver in her decision.

Her repugnance towards Charles was well founded; for three years he had not ceased to devastate her beloved country, and under the specious pretext of obtaining guardianship of her person to which he had a right, he had sought by violence to make her captive.

According to old d'Argentré, Anne's heart was exceedingly "haut et indomptable," and for many days all the lords of her Council, won over by Louis Duc d'Orleans and the Comte de Dunois, whom Charles had sent for the purpose, tried in vain to make her hear reason, and Françoise de Dinan was obliged to have recourse to the influence of her confessor, to point out to her that God demanded she should make this sacrifice for the happiness of her country. Religion gained the day, and the girl was conquered. Charles then lost no time, under the pretext of a pilgrimage, to repair with his whole Court to a chapel of

A Twice Crowned Queen

Nôtre Dame, near the gates of Rennes. His devotions ended, he suddenly entered the town, accompanied by Anne de Beaujeu, his sister, the Comte de Dunois, a hundred armed men, and fifty yeomen of his guard.

The following day he begged for a private interview with the young Duchess, which lasted a long time. Three days afterwards, the ceremony of their betrothal took place in the chapel of Nôtre Dame, in presence of the Duc d'Orleans and the Seigneur Dunois on Charles' side; and of the Prince d'Orange and many Breton nobles on that of the Duchess.

Charles must have had great charm and fascination, and also wonderful tact, to have succeeded in so short a space of time in bringing the headstrong little Duchess to his feet, and if it were not for the excuse of her youth she would deserve great blame for so entirely throwing aside her betrothal to Maximilian, a betrothal which, till she listened to Charles, she had looked upon as a binding marriage contract. No doubt the fact of Charles being on the spot and able to plead his own cause had much to do with his success, and the thought of at once becoming Queen over one of the most powerful kingdoms of Europe, cannot fail to have influenced one so ambitious as Anne.

The Maréchal de Polhain, who had been chosen by Maximilian to represent him at his betrothal with Anne, hearing rumours of this new and unexpected alliance, made inquiries of the French and Breton lords he met, but could not get any information confirming it. A few days afterwards, he was invited to the wedding ceremony, which was to take place in Touraine, at the Castle of Langeais. He, naturally, refused to attend, and—as there was no longer any doubt of the truth of the rumour—hastened to Mechlin, to inform his master of what had happened.

The whole of Europe was taken aback by this sudden and unforeseen alliance ; for besides the reasons which existed against Anne's marriage to the French King, it was well-known that since the conclusion of the treaty of Arras, in 1482, between Louis XI. and Maximilian, Charles himself, then Dauphin, had been solemnly betrothed to Maximilian's daughter, Margaret of Austria. The actual ceremony took place a few days before the death of Louis XI. at Amboise, whither the little princess of three years old had been sent. In the presence of a crowd of spectators, in the public square of the town, Charles, a boy of twelve, had consented to take Margaret as his wife. The marriage took place the same day in the lower chapel of the Castle in the presence of Anne de Beaujeu, the Sire de la Trémoille, the Comte de Dunois, the Sire d'Albret, and many deputies from the chief provincial towns. The Dauphin, clad in a robe of white damask, lined with black velvet, had married the little princess with his hand and ring. A Mass was said, after which the young Dauphin thanked all who were present.*

After Louis XI.'s death, Margaret of Austria was looked upon as Queen, and treated with the honour due to her rank, until Charles suddenly put an end to the whole affair by marrying Anne. Never had there been such flagrant violations of pledges given and re-

* *Mémoires de Philippe de Commynes.*

ceived! The Austrian Court published a document in Latin, in which it denounced the injuries it had received at the hands of France, and caused a report to be spread abroad that the Duchess was not free to contract this alliance, and that she had only consented to it after being carried off.* This report was so far believed, that the Pope, on granting the dispensation—asked for after the marriage—formally declared that he would only confirm the union on being assured that it was not preceded by a violent seizure of Anne's person. The young Duchess herself, determined to refute this calumny, stated before an ecclesiastical court that she had suffered no violence, and that she had come to Langeais of her own free will and pleasure, there to marry Charles VIII.†

In the interval between the betrothal and the marriage, François Comte de Dunois and de Longueville, died suddenly from an attack of apoplexy whilst riding from Nantes to Tours.

---

* Diplomatic negotiations between France and Austria during the first thirty years of the sixteenth century.

† Declaration attached to the marriage-contract of Anne of Brittany and Charles VIII. (Lobineau).

A Twice Crowned Queen

The Bretons, feeling that this marriage with Charles VIII. had placed their country completely in the hands of France, looked upon the death of the Comte de Dunois as a bad omen.

Jean Molinet says that there were three things of great wonder in this alliance : (1) that Charles VIII. should have had the audacity to do it, having already publicly married Maximilian's daughter; (2) that the Duchess of Brittany should have accepted as a husband this inveterate enemy of her house; (3) that, to the superstitious fear of the whole people, the Seigneur de Dunois, who had done so much to effect this union, should have fallen from his horse and died on returning from the ceremony of betrothal.

On the 24th of August 1490, soon after Anne's arrival at Rennes, her young sister, Isabeau, aged twelve, fell ill and died. One cannot but feel deeply for Anne at losing her only and much loved sister, from whom she had never been separated, who had played and studied with her, and shared her joys and sorrows.

CHAPTER II

THE Castle of Langeais, where the nuptials of
Charles and Anne took place, was built under
the superintendence of Jean Bourré, a lover of
art, especially in the form of architecture, and a
favourite of Louis XI. who, in 1465, bestowed
on him the Captainry of Langeais. Though
severe and simple in style, it stands out among
the many châteaux of Touraine with a majestic
beauty of its own ; and here, towards the end of
November 1490, the Duchess was conducted,
having left Rennes secretly, guarded by three
members of her household. Never did she
look more happy and charming than when she

34

descended from her travelling coach, clad in a
robe of black satin and velvet, and a costly
cloak of velvet, trimmed with one hundred
and thirty-nine skins of sable.

In spite of the poverty of her Treasury, Anne
provided luxuriously for this journey, and it is
probable that the Estates of Brittany granted
her a generous subsidy so that she might appear
in a manner befitting her exalted position. An
account of the expenses she incurred for her entry
into France has come down to us.* Among the
articles mentioned are two camp beds, one of them
—fairly simple—was draped with black, white,
and violet damask, and its canopy was lined with
red taffetas. The materials, of which the
number of yards for each part is given (without
the cost of making up), were worth about
14,000 francs ; the other, still richer, was composed of a canopy, curtains, and hangings of
crimson cloth, embroidered in gold with
festoons and cords of violet cloth of gold,
bordered with a heavy fringe of black silk ; the
canopy, festoons, and curtains were lined with
blue taffetas. The price of these various stuffs

* *Archives de Nantes.*

exceeded the sum of 108,000 francs. For the trappings of the horses and hangings of the chariots, twelve yards of black velvet and three of crimson were used. Anne's travelling dress, already mentioned, cost 60,740 francs.

The marriage contract was signed in one of the great halls of the Castle, on the 6th December 1491, and the wedding ceremony took place the same day with the usual pomp displayed on such occasions.

Fair as Anne looked on her arrival, her appearance on this day must have been still more striking; her wedding dress was made of cloth of gold overlaid with designs in high relief, which gave to this material the name of "drap d'or-trait-enlevé," one yard of cloth costing 7350 francs; at first this over-robe was edged with fine skins of the black lamb of Lombardy, but this fur not being considered rich enough, it was changed for sable. The entire dress, without the making up, did not cost less than £5250.

Anne also gave dresses to the courtiers and servants who accompanied her to France; Jean de Châlons and Françoise de Dinan were

included in this distribution, the Prince receiving cloth of gold, and Françoise, violet velvet;
the maids of honour were given dresses of tan-
coloured velvet or satin.

Anne being, since the death of her sister, sole
heiress to one of the largest duchies of Europe,
the inheritance she brought to Charles was of
enormous gain to France, and it made the
contract drawn up at the time of her marriage
of great importance for the future of the two
parties. All the eminent personages of the two
Courts were present at its signing, among them,
on the side of France, being Louis Duc
d'Orleans, Pierre Duc de Bourbon, Charles
Comte d'Angoulême, and Guy de Rochefort,
Chancellor of France; on the side of Brittany
were, Jean de Châlons, Prince d'Orange,
Philippe de Montauban, Chancellor of Brittany,
the Sire de Coetquen, the Sire de Guémenée,
and many other lords of the House of Rohan.
It was stipulated in this contract that the
two parties having equal claims to the Duchy
of Brittany, and wishing to put an end to the
war which for many years had desolated the
country, had resolved to contract a marriage;

that the Duchess Anne, in consideration of the
honour which Charles VIII. conferred upon her
in wedding her, gave up to him entire possession of the Duchy, without the power of revok-
ing this gift in her will, should she not survive
her lord the King. On his side, Charles VIII.,
if he died before the Duchess without leaving
an heir by her, yielded up all rights he claimed
to have over the Duchy of Brittany ; nevertheless, to avoid the recurrence of wars and
"sinistres fortunes," which had just come to an
end, the Duchess bound herself never to marry
again except with the successor of the King, her
husband, or the heir of this successor. It was
further stipulated that the Duchess should receive
the same dowry that the mother of Charles VIII.
had enjoyed ; that all the furniture and jewels, of
whatever price they might be, that she should
have in her possession on the King's death should
be her property, according to his wish. The
Prince d'Orange, on hearing of the above conditions, approved of them entirely, and gave up
to the Duchess all his rights over Brittany.*

* Traite de Mariage, etc., *Historiens de Charles VIII.*
(Godefroi.)

A Twice Crowned Queen

Such was this famous deed, and, strange to say, within a few years, improbable as most of its clauses seem, they were all of them fulfilled.

Soon after the marriage, preparations were made for the return of Charles to Paris, and accompanied by his young wife he left the Castle of Langeais, stopping at many towns on the way. The Queen was received with great magnificence; joy was universal among high and low, rich and poor, for all agreed in thinking this union a most desirable one.

Anne was crowned at Saint Denis on the 8th of February 1492. She was dressed in a robe of damask or white satin, her dark plaited hair fell over her shoulders, and fresh and gracious she must have looked as she sat on the dais set up in the choir of the church. After she was anointed and crowned, a solemn Mass was said, and during the benediction, Louis Duc d'Orleans held the crown of France over her head because it was too large and heavy for her. By her side stood the Duchesse de Bourbon, and many other ladies, each wearing a coronet as the badge of their rank.*

* St. Gelais de Monlieu, *Histoire de Louis XII.*, Paris, 1622.

39

A Twice Crowned Queen

The day after her coronation, the Queen made a solemn entry into Paris; members of Parliament, lords of Justice, all the civil and military officers of the Châtelet, the Provost of Paris, the Provost of the merchants, the sheriffs and Corporation of the town followed by the most distinguished citizens, flocked to meet her in their State costumes. "Truly," adds the chronicler who gives us these details, "when everybody had assembled, such a marvellous crowd of people had formed, that from the chapel, all along the route, and in all the streets up to the palace, one could not turn."*

Anne, now in all the freshness of her youthful beauty, soon gained great ascendency over Charles. From her infancy she had been treated with the respect due to a sovereign princess, and she could not bear the slightest opposition to her wishes. Those around her soon found out that they had no weak tool to deal with, and she herself was determined not to be a puppet in anyone's hands. Anne de Bourbon, her sister-in-law, soon had bitter experience of this: "She wished," says

* St. Gelais de Monlieu.

40

A Twice Crowned Queen

Brantôme, "to make use of some prerogative and authority on her side, but she met with her match, for the Queen was a shrewd Bretonne, very proud and haughty with regard to her equals, therefore Madame de Bourbon had to yield, and give place to the Queen." *

Paris, strange to say, had no attraction for the young Queen; doubtless the luxury and stiffness of its Court life were too great a contrast to the simplicity and open-air existence of her dear Brittany, therefore Charles hastened to direct that the Castle of Amboise, where he usually lived, and for which he had a great affection, should be prepared, at no matter what cost, for the reception of his young bride. Additions to the building were made which almost doubled its size; furniture, tapestries, linen, and plate were completely renewed, as is shown in the account of expenses incurred on this occasion. The first part of the account is devoted to the cloth of gold or silk which was required for the chapel or the apartments of the Castle. Under this heading were included precious stuffs and

* *Dames Illustres.*

tapestries made not only in France, but in Turkey and Flanders, and which served as hangings; thousands of yards, costing more than £10,000, were used. Past and contemporary events were portrayed on the tapestries. André Denisot and Guillaume Ménagier, workers of Tours, had charge of the furnishing; one room by Ménagier was hung with silk tapestry, on which the history of Moses was represented, and the floor was covered with a large, fine silk Moorish carpet. Other portions of the same account relate to table and house linen, to the silver services for the use of the King, and the pewter ones for the kitchen, to furniture of all kinds—bedsteads, chests, tables, footstools, and benches. In the list of furniture we find an oak table, fifteen feet long, with a bench of the same length for the Queen's dining-room, and two sideboards for the service of the pages; two wooden bedsteads, six feet long and six wide for the room of the maids of honour, a table for the Queen's doctors, and a bed, six feet wide by six and a half long; two caskets, one for the Queen's room and the other for that of the Princess of

Tarento. The colours Charles VIII. preferred were red and yellow, and these prevailed in the four rooms of the King's suite. Three fleur-de-lis in yellow thread was the mark on all the sheets which, to the number of seven or eight hundred dozen, stocked the linen room of the Castle.

In the galleries at Amboise was to be seen a collection of historic armour and weapons, which had belonged to the most famous kings of France or to celebrated warriors. The preservation of these arms had become a custom of late years in France, and among those in the Castle were the axe of King Clovis, the sword of Dagobert, the dagger of Charlemagne, two axes belonging to St. Louis, the sword of Philippe-le-bel, that of King John, two swords of Charles VII., four swords and a dagger which had belonged to Louis XI. In 1495, two swords which Charles VIII. used at the battle of Fornova were added to the collection. Among the weapons which belonged to famous warriors, was the three-cornered axe of Bertrand du Guesclin, and the armour worn at the coronation of Charles

VII. by Jeanne d'Arc ; the helmet, to which is
attached a gorget of mail, was gilded outside
and lined with crimson satin.* This armour
was given to the Maid of Orleans by Charles
VII., and the artist who, by Anne's order,
painted the miniatures for her copy of Antoine
Dufour's *Femmes Célebres* has depicted the
heroine in this very armour, riding on a white
horse, caparisoned in red and gold.

Everything in the Castle was made of the
best material with a view of lasting many
years ; workmanship—which in the absence
of machinery was purely manual—was also of
the best. Artists were quite content to spend
years over the production of a fine painting
or piece of sculpture. Quality—not quantity
—was expected in those days, and it is quite
certain that future generations will not have
the same beautiful works of art handed down
to them from the present time.

Nothing was more natural than that Charles
should have furnished the Castle of Amboise
with the greatest luxury for the young and

* Extract from an inventory made at Amboise on the 23rd
September 1499.

gracious bride who, in marrying him, had brought such a precious jewel as Brittany to adorn the Crown of France.

In fact, this eventful union astonished the whole of Europe, and it is said that Lorenzo de Medici, on hearing the news, exclaimed : "Oh, what a powerful monarchy is France!" * Henry VII., King of England, Ferdinand II., King of Spain, and Maximilian of Austria, King of the Romans, united their efforts to humble France, but this formidable league was soon broken up. Henry VII., hearing that Charles had bought over the King of Spain by restoring Cerdagne and le Roussillon, without even demanding the 300,000 gold crowns which Louis XI. had advanced on these provinces after besieging Boulogne, hastened to make peace on condition of receiving a pecuniary indemnity for the expenses which this war in Brittany had cost him. Maximilian, the most seriously injured, alone remained ; by the same blow he had lost Anne of Brittany whom he regarded as his lawful wife, and his daughter had lost a

* Daru, *Histoire de Bretagne*.

husband. The only compensation for this
double injury was the possession of the two
fine provinces of Artois and Burgundy, which
the Princess, his daughter, had received as
dowry. Margaret, after a stay of twelve years
at the Court of France, where she had lived as
future Queen, was sent back to her father.
Charles took care she should be treated with
every respect, and Anne showed great sympathy, trying by every means to make up to
her for the great injury from which she was
suffering. When she was about to depart, the
Queen ordered the most skilful of her maids of
honour, Jeanne de Jambes, Dame de Beaumont,
to embroider a head ornament to present to
Margaret, which together with other jewels in
gold weighed four hundred and fifty lbs.

On the 12th of June 1492 she started on her
return to Austria, accompanied by the French
nobles who had been attached to her suite while
in her adopted country. They were much distressed, and did all in their power to distract
her, and show how great was their sympathy.
The Princess bore herself with dignity, and was
as calm as she was a few years later, when, on

her way to Spain to marry the Prince of the Asturias,—part of her fleet destroyed in a tremendous gale, and her own vessel about to founder,—she wrote the following epitaph :—

> "Ci gist Margot, la gentil damoiselle
> Qu'a deux maris, et encore est pucelle,"

which fortunately was not needed, for she arrived safely at the port of Santander in March 1497. She was annoyed, however, when on passing through the town of Arras the people gave her a purely French cheer, " Noël, Noël ! "   She said to them, " Do not cry ' Noël,' but ' Vive Bourgogne ! ' " *   Although Margaret always bore a grudge against France, she many times showed much respect and affection for Anne, and after she was appointed Ruler of the Netherlands, and Anne had married Louis xii., she increased her attentions, which were eagerly reciprocated by the French Queen. Diplomatic papers of this period are full of civilities exchanged between the two princesses.

* Le Clay, *Correspondence de Maximilien et de Marguerite d'Autriche.*

A Twice Crowned Queen

Charles VIII.'s early life was spent at Amboise, where he seems to have been kept like a prisoner within the precincts of the Castle, for Claude Seyssel tells us that no one was allowed to visit him, not even nobles and officers of State passing through the town. On one occasion, however, by order of Louis XI., the Seigneur du Bouchage visited the Dauphin, and doubtless pitying the poor boy's dull life, thought he might be allowed to go outside the town to shoot a few partridges. When the King heard of this he was much annoyed, and from that time Du Bouchage fell into disgrace.

Louis evidently desired to keep Charles, not only from knowledge of the world, but of the duties which education alone could fit him for. The only Latin he would allow him to learn, Brantôme says, was his own favourite maxim, " Qui nescit dissimulare, nescit regnare." * It is certain, however, that the " Rosier de Guerres " was composed for the education of Charles VIII. According to Lacroix du Maine, Louis himself was the author of this book, but it is far more probable that it was written at his command

* *Vies des Hommes Illustres.*

48

A Twice Crowned Queen

by Etienne Porchier.*   His mother, Charlotte
of Savoy, a woman of fine and cultivated
mind, taught him to read and write, and
we can picture her seated at one of the
windows of the fine old Castle on the banks of
the Loire, with her little son by her side, trying
to impart to him some of her own bright intelligence, and reading stories about great men
and their brave and noble deeds.

He was only twelve years old when he
ascended the throne, so he was able, to some
extent, to make up for lost time, and one of his
historians tells us in a characteristic way that
" After the death of Louis, when he had taken
upon himself the royal dignity, he began
eagerly to read books written in the French
language, and wished also to learn Latin.†
His favourite studies were still the deeds of
heroes and conquerors, of Cæsar and Charlemagne in particular, which filled his young
mind with dreams of glory ; and these ideas
were also encouraged by the tournaments and
warlike exercises of the age, in which he took

* *Manuscrits Français de la Bibliothèque de Paris.*
† Pierre Defrey, *Chroniques du Roi Charles VIII.*

great delight, until he seems to have imagined himself some hero of romance destined for a great and perilous achievement.*

He afterwards gave excellent proof of his love for art and letters, by presenting France with beautiful pictures, statues, and books; and by encouraging learned men, artists, and skilled workers of every kind to settle in his kingdom; he was wont to say that the "sword and the lance were offensive weapons, the cuirass and the shield defensive ones, but that letters were offensive and defensive at the same time." †

For some time after his marriage, Charles devoted himself entirely to his young wife, and they never left each other, living either at Amboise or at the Castle of Plessis-les-Tours, which had also been enlarged and richly furnished. When affairs of State obliged the King to journey, Anne either accompanied him or went to meet him in towns where he had to stay. So young a wife about to become a mother was in need of every care, so if he had to go anywhere in haste, she

---

* Sismondi, *Histoire des Français*.
† Cimber, *Archives Curieuses*.

followed by easy stages, often preferring the journey by water. On 8th January 1492 she went by boat from Melun to Paris, accompanied by the Seigneur de la Trémoille and many others. To wile away the time, she played at a game called "Flux" with fifty gold crowns. In the list of expenses incurred on her journeys, it is thus given: "A Elle, la somme de cinquante escus d'or au soleil, à elle baillée et delivrée comptant et en ses mains par ce present tresorier, le huitieme jour dud. moys de Janvier, oud. an, pour jouer au fleuz en son bateau en la rivière de Seine," etc.

Great was the joy of Charles and of the whole of France and Brittany when, on the 10th of October 1492, eleven months after the marriage, Anne gave birth to a son at the Castle of Plessis. She was scarcely fifteen, and every precaution had been taken for a happy result of her first confinement. Furniture, linen, plate, and provisions of all kinds had been sent to the Castle. Arnoul de Viviers, a skilful goldsmith,—attached to the household of the ex-Regent, Anne de Beaujeu,

—was sent from Moulins to Tours, in order to make certain vessels and other articles of gold to be used on this occasion.

The King, proud and happy, hastened to write the good news to the Ministers of Foreign Courts, in the following words :—

"Our trusty and well-beloved friends, thanks to God and Our Lady, about four o'clock in the morning, our very dear and much loved consort, the Queen, gave birth to a fine son, of which event we wish to inform you with all speed, as our good servants, who we know will much rejoice at this," etc.*

The Dauphin's baptism took place three days afterwards, on the 13th of October, with great pomp and ceremony in the chapel of the Castle. His godfathers, the Duc d'Orleans and the Duc de Bourbon, and his godmother, the Queen of Sicily, Jeanne de Laval, widow of René d'Anjou, were robed completely in cloth of gold. The Duc de Nemours carried the wax candle, the Comte de Foix the gold salt-cellar, the Duc de Vendôme the ewer, the Dauphin of Spain, Anne's uncle, the basin and

* *Historiens de Charles VIII.*

towel. Jean de Châlons, Prince d'Orange, bareheaded, and wearing a long robe of cloth of gold, carried the newborn child. Madame l'Amirale, widow of Louis, Bastard of Bourbon, carried the holy Chrism in a vial ornamented with precious stones of the rarest value. The Duchesses of Bourbon and Orleans, followed by the lords and ladies of the Court, walked behind the Queen of Sicily. Such was the pompous cortège which went to join the King, who was waiting devoutly in the chapel with the priest who was to perform the ceremony. He was a simple Franciscan friar, already famous for his holy life, the founder of the Minim Order in France, and afterwards canonised under the name of St. François de Paule. We are told by the chronicler, that during the ceremony the King "ne cessa pas de tenir la main du saint homme." *

The Dauphin was given the name of Charles-Orland, and here we have a proof of the exalted state of the King's imagination in calling his firstborn son after the celebrated hero of Roncesvalles.

* Godefroi.

A Twice Crowned Queen

Needless to say, this precious child was the object of the most solicitous care. Placed under the protection of the Virgin, he was always dressed in white (*voué au blanc*) covered with cloth of silver. When he was a little older, his mother ordered Jean Martel, a gold-smith of Tours, to make him a silver-gilt rattle with shells.

All this tender care for their child did not prevent the young parents from leaving him at a very early age for the city of Lyons, where preparations were going on for that adventurous expedition into Italy of which I shall speak in the next chapter. Before quitting Amboise, however, Charles took care to leave the most minute instructions in writing as to the precautions which the governors of the Dauphin were to take, not only for the defence of his person, but for the preservation of his health. A hundred men of the Scotch Guard were to watch continually at the gates of the town and Castle. No shooting was to be allowed in the neighbourhood; one of the four chamberlains was always to remain at the door of the Tower in which the child's

apartments were, as was the custom when
the King was Dauphin. If a stranger came
to lodge either in the town or its immediate
neighbourhood, the landlord was at once
obliged to give notice to the Scotch Guard.
If any disease was prevalent, no one from
outside was allowed to enter the town. When
the venerable François de Paule wished to
visit the Prince, he was never to be accompanied by more than one monk, and he must
be of French birth, and one who had never
visited the kingdom of Naples. Charles seems
to have feared the plots and poisons of the
Italians, on whom he was so soon going to
make war. The governors were to give the
King news of Monseigneur as often as possible,
at the very least once a fortnight. If they
needed more soldiers for the guard, they were
to summon the nobles and bowmen of Touraine
and Berry, whom the King had ordered to
hold themselves in readiness. If through any
infectious malady the governors of the Dauphin
had to take him away from Amboise, they
were to choose one of the most secure castles
in Touraine. If it was thought necessary to

take the child for a walk, in a litter or otherwise, he was always to be accompanied by the greatest number of archers available.

In spite of the affection which Charles VIII. felt for Anne, he would never let her take any part in public affairs. Some historians, doubtless with the object of flattering the memory of this Princess, have asserted that by a secret article of her marriage contract, she had reserved to herself the public and civil administration of her Duchy. This is an error, for during the years from 1492–1498 all the acts of Brittany are given in the name of Charles VIII., and not in that of his wife.* The King, small in stature, but great in courage and very firm, would not let himself be ruled by a young princess, who, with remarkable intelligence and vivacious but obstinate character, never failed to submit to the wishes of a husband she loved.

* Dom Morice, *Preuves de l'Histoire de Bretagne*.

CHAPTER III

IT may seem strange that Charles VIII.—
triumphant and absolute master of Brittany
—should have been so lenient with his adversaries, Henry VII., Maximilian, and Ferdinand
of Spain, and made such large concessions to
purchase their reconciliation ; but his mind was
dominated by visions of military glory, and the
thought of a noble and chivalrous enterprise
which was to end in the capture of Constantinople and the recovery of the Holy Sepulchre.
He wished first to dictate laws to Italy, and
laid claim to the crown of Naples, making use
of the rights his father had left him over that
kingdom, Sicily and Jerusalem. His claim to
the kingdom of Naples was derived originally

from a bequest in the will of René, Comte de Provence, which excluded the son of his own daughter, the rightful heir of the house of Anjou. Charles was surrounded by a crowd of young and valiant knights, who urged him on to these fatal enterprises, and made him forget the happiness and prosperity of France.

In vain did Anne, with that good sense and prudence which always distinguished her, try to show the folly of such undertakings. He paid no heed to her advice, nor to that of his sister, Anne de Beaujeu. "Nothing essential to the conduct of a war was at hand," says Commynes, "the King was very young, weak in health, headstrong in will, surrounded by few wise counsellors, and wholly destitute of the requisite funds."

Early in the year 1494, Charles and Anne, followed by a numerous and brilliant Court, journeyed to Lyons, where they made a State entry, for neither of them had visited the town before. One may judge of the pomp and magnificence displayed on this occasion by the following details which concern the Queen. Six pages clad in crimson velvet embroidered with the letter "A" in gold thread, and with caps of the same, preceded her; she herself was seated in a swaying chariot, covered with crimson velvet embroidered with the letter "A" in gold and ermine, which was drawn by six steeds caparisoned like the chariot. Her ladies-in-waiting followed her; then came the mule which the Queen usually rode, decked in black and gold cloth, edged with white and gold fringe; the harness was of white silk and gold cord with tassels of the same, and the large saddle was of crimson satin; the State litter, borne by two mules—one in front and one behind—was covered with Frisian cloth of gold.

The Queen wore a short-waisted dress of cloth of gold trimmed with ermine and fastened by diamond buttons. Her gold girdle and Breton cap of silk and gold were ornamented with precious stones. A long mantle of red velvet lined with ermine fell from her shoulders to the ground.

Charles stayed some time at Lyons, and prepared himself for the expedition into Italy by the warlike sports in favour at that period.

A Twice Crowned Queen

Guillaume de Jaligny, an eye-witness of these
games, gives us the following account : " At
that time at Lyons, jousts, tournaments, tiltings
at the ring, and other pleasant feats of arms
which had not been seen there before, very
frequently took place ; Monseigneur d'Orleans
took part in all of them, and was always one of
the first to challenge, as if he wished with all
his might to give pleasure to the King as much
and more than anyone else of the company.
These sports took place in the streets of the
town, and tiers of seats were erected at the
crossways. The greatest of the jousts generally happened in the Rue de la Juiverie,
because the knights in quest of adventure
found the finest and best there, according to
what they desired."

The King himself also took part in these
diversions. Several of the garments and the
armour which he wore on this expedition were
made at Lyons. Among the garments was a
sort of tunic, open at the sides, and with large
sleeves, called a "journade," which the King
was to wear over his armour. It was of white
satin lined with silk, and bordered with scarlet

A Twice Crowned Queen

cloth of gold, with a fringe in gold thread as long as one's finger, the whole coat being embroidered in gold; there was also a white plume, composed of large and small feathers attached with gold threads and ornamented with jewels.

The mounts reserved for the King were seven in number. These had been given to him by the Provost of Paris, the Seneschal d'Armagnac, the Admiral de Graville, and other friends. One called "la Quintaine" was a present from Anne herself, and its trappings were of black leather covered with velvet.

About the same time Anne made State entries into other important towns, and passing through Moulins on the 16th of May, she gave liberty to a knight who was imprisoned there.* On Saturday the 23rd of August 1494, Charles, accompanied by the Queen and many princes, lords, ladies and maids of honour, made a magnificent entry into the town of Grenoble. The principal streets were hung with tapestries, and very fine mysteries were represented in honour of the King and

* *Régistres criminels du Parlement de Paris.*

Queen. The festivities lasted six days, during which time Charles and his wife lived in the little palace where the parliament of Dauphiné was held.

The baggage for the expedition to Italy, brought so far by heavy waggons, was now placed on mules in order to cross the Alps. The march this expedition was to follow was regulated with the utmost care and in a definite manner; the lodgings of the King and the army were arranged by the Grand Marshal, Pierre de Valetaut, who knew the country well; several of the King's stewards were sent on in advance to the principal towns where he was to stop, and with them were lawyers and orators who should be able to speak on this affair if it was necessary. Special ambassadors were sent to the Italian princes; La Trémoille to the King of the Romans, Louis Lucas to Lodovico il Moro at Milan, d'Aubigny to Rome, and Philippe de Commynes to Venice.

The princes and people of Northern Italy awaited with impatience the march of Charles VIII. against the King of Naples, for it was generally thought that this expedition, announced

long ago by religious prophecies, would be the
beginning of the famous crusade against the
Turks, preached and acclaimed throughout
Europe since the taking of Constantinople by
Mahomet II. in 1453. With this intention,
dear to the Christian Church, Pope Innocent
VIII. had made a special appeal to the King of
France by encouraging him to recover possession of the kingdom of Naples in the name of
the House of Anjou; but Alexander VI., who
had succeeded Innocent, hindered and prevented the enterprise as being contrary to the
interests of the Holy See, or rather to his own
interests. The republics of Genoa, Florence,
and Venice had been friendly with the late
King Ferdinand of Naples, but fearing the
ambitious schemes of his son Alfonso, they
solicited the intervention of the French army.

On Friday the 29th of August, Charles VIII.,
after having heard Mass, bade farewell to
Anne, and left Grenoble on his way towards
Italy. The Queen was thus for the first time
separated from a husband she considered one
of the greatest kings on earth. With sorrow
she saw him depart on a most adventurous

A Twice Crowned Queen

expedition; she knew him to be brave to rash-
ness, and she had heard sinister accounts of
Italy, therefore she had everything to fear and
little to hope from this extravagant project.
In her exaltation as a Breton and a Christian
we see her constantly engaged in prayer and
almsgiving; the principal churches of Brittany,
Touraine, Ile-de-France, and Lyonnais received
numberless offerings for the celebration of
Masses; she sent two candles, weighing twenty
pounds each, to the royal abbey of Saint Denis,
which were to burn—the first before the statue,
the second before the shrine of that powerful
protector; she gave £40 to the Brotherhood
of the Minims, recently established at Tours
by François de Paule, for the Masses they had
said, and a bell to the convent of Nôtre-Dame-
des-Anges, at Lyons, as a thank-offering for
the zeal of the monks in praying for the King.
She did not spare herself; every day she heard
Mass and other offices to beg God to protect
the King and his army; her alms, more
abundant than ever, were distributed to all
those who implored her help. One day, as she
was passing through Roanne, on her way from

64

Lyons to Moulins, she met a poor sick soldier, and eagerly succoured him.

The prayers of the Queen and her people were granted. The King's conquests were as rapid as they were marvellous. Anne could not hear without pride of the exploits of many brave Bretons, and of her husband's triumphant entry into Naples; but it is a little surprising, that for about fifteen months, while the expedition to Italy lasted, Anne never returned to Amboise to see her son. She remained the whole time either at Lyons or Moulins with her sister-in-law, Anne de Beaujeu. No doubt she obeyed the commands of her husband, who wished her to be as near him as possible, and where they could more quickly get news of one another. It is certain that nearly every day Anne wrote to Charles, and constantly received replies from him, according to his orders sending couriers in all directions. But the joys of triumph were of short duration; a year had scarcely passed since the King had left France, when bad news came. Charles had failed to make good his conquests; his army was decimated by sickness and the pleasures in-

E

A Twice Crowned Queen

separable from victory; the Italian princes, at
first his allies, had turned against him, and
together with the Venetians, Maximilian's Germans, and the King of Aragon's Spaniards, had
just formed a formidable league, with the object
of destroying what remained of his army.

The Queen was eager for Charles to return,
and perhaps she was aware of the follies and
excesses into which he had allowed himself
to be drawn under the influence of Italian
manners. She was also uneasy at the dangers
of all kinds which beset him in a country
which was every day becoming more hostile
to France.

After a rapid march from the south, Charles
descended from the Apennines on the 6th of
July 1495, and arrived at the village of
Fornova with 9000 men in fighting condition.
Here he encountered the allied forces under
Gonzaga, Marquis of Mantua, whose numbers
exceeded 35,000. After some fruitless negotiations the King gave the order for attack, and
boldly charged this multitude, gaining a brilliant
victory; 3500 of the enemy were either slain
or drowned in the river Taro.

66

A Twice Crowned Queen

Commynes, who was present at this battle, renders more justice to Charles than he usually does, but the courage displayed by the "little King" on this occasion is confirmed by all who saw him.

"On Monday morning about seven o'clock, on the 6th of July 1495, the noble King mounted his horse and summoned me several times. I came to him and found him completely armed, and mounted on the finest horse I have ever seen in my life, called 'Savoy' (many say that it was from Brescia; it was black, and had only one eye; and though it was small, it was a good size for him who rode it); and it seemed that this young man was quite different to what nature had made him both in size and bearing; for he was very timid in speech and is so still (he had been brought up in great fear, and with people of small account), and this horse made him look big, and his face was handsome and of a good colour, and his speech bold and wise."

Three months later, on the 9th of November 1495, Charles arrived in safety at Lyons after a memorable expedition, which, though crowned with success, only paved the way for disastrous wars in the two following reigns.

Anxieties connected with the war in Italy were still unallayed when sorrow of another kind smote the heart of Anne of Brittany. The Dauphin's health had never been particularly good, and the chamberlains appointed to watch over him were to inform the Queen and her husband of the smallest circumstance likely to injure it. In August 1495, Charles, then at Turin, received a letter informing him that the smallpox was raging at Amboise, and that his instructions in the matter were awaited. The King gave orders that doctors were to be summoned in order to know whether the Dauphin was running any risk. Olivier Laurens, Bernard Chaussade, Jean Michel, and many other doctors assembled, and after consultation they replied that there had been smallpox at Amboise but that it was nearly over, moreover, they had been informed that great care had been taken to prevent the townspeople from communicating with the Castle, and that they were not of opinion that the child's residence should be changed. Anne,

slightly reassured, sent a courier to the King.
She also wrote a letter to Madame de Buffières,
governess of the Dauphin, thanking her for the
care she had taken over her son's health.*
Alas! it was not long before she received the
most alarming news, and soon after she heard
that the Dauphin had died on the 6th of
December, in the beginning of his fourth year.
"A fine child," says Commynes, "bold in
speech, and fearing not the things other children
are usually frightened at." He adds with his
ordinary malice, that this precocity of which
the absent Charles had not given proof, was
the reason why the father bore his mourning so
easily. Anne, too, has been accused of heart-
lessness in staying away from her son so long,
but we must remember that her position was
a difficult one. She could not bring herself to
leave the husband she adored in the midst of
danger, and though she could not accompany
him to Italy, she could at least remain near the
frontier, ready at any moment to receive him
if he were wounded, or else to go to him and
nurse him with tender care. Also, the distance

* Vatout, *Histoires des Résidences Royales.*

was great from Lyons to Amboise, and journeys in those days were no small undertaking, especially for royalties, who could not move without an enormous following.

Brantôme is more charitable than Commynes, and explains the seeming unconcern of Charles at his son's death in the following way : " After the death of the Dauphin, King Charles and his Queen were full of such desolate grief that the doctors, fearing the weakness and feeble constitution of the King, were of opinion that excess of sorrow might be prejudicial to his health ; they therefore advised as many distractions as possible, and suggested that the princes at Court should invent new pastimes, dances, and mummeries to give pleasure to the King and Queen, which being done, the Monseigneur d'Orleans devised a masquerade with dances, in which he danced with such gaiety and so played the fool that the Queen thought he was making merry because he was nearer the throne of France, seeing that the Dauphin was dead. She was extremely displeased, and looked on him with such aversion that he was obliged to leave Amboise, where the Court then was, and go to his Castle of Blois."

About the same time Louis d'Orleans met with another misfortune in the death of his first cousin, Charles Comte d'Angoulême, who, hearing of the death of the Dauphin, had hastened to go to Court to present his condolence to the King; but on the way from Cognac to Châteauneuf he suffered so much from the cold, that he was attacked the same night with paralysis, followed quickly by tertian fever. His wife, Louise de Savoie, cared for him day and night till his death. This good Prince, feeling his end approaching, appointed Louis the guardian and protector of his wife and children, "humbly praying him so to be because all his life he had held him to be his special friend and seigneur, and of all men he had in him the greatest trust." He gave up his soul to God on the 1st of January 1496. Louis Duc d'Orleans mourned deeply for his cousin, "whom he loved with great and perfect affection above all other." A faithful servant of the late Charles d'Angoulême spoke thus of the noble and touching conduct of the Duc

d'Orleans : "From that time he took the
mother and children under his protection,
sustaining them and managing all their affairs
as though they were his very own, and bestow-
ing so many benefits and honours upon them,
that father, husband, son or brother could not
have acted more generously."

Louis d'Orleans retained the favour of the
King notwithstanding the Queen's ill-will
towards him, and whatever influence she may
have used to get him sent back to Italy, she
could not take from him his title of Heir-
presumptive to the Crown.

In the three years following the death of the
Dauphin, two sons and a daughter were born,
but they all died in their infancy. In vain did
Anne take every precaution to save the lives of
these little creatures whom death snatched from
her so ruthlessly. She summoned nurses from
Brittany, and the superstitious beliefs of her
own country came back to her mind. She
presented them with amulets, a Guienne
crown-piece wrapped up in paper, a piece of
black wax in a bag of cloth of gold, six
serpents' tongues,—a large one, two of medium

size, and three little ones,—and rosaries of
chalcedony and jasper ; she not only sent votive
offerings to the venerated shrines of the saints
in Brittany, and presented rich gifts every year
to the Holy Virgin of Auray, but she went
herself on a pilgrimage.   Alas ! it was all to no
purpose ; a relentless fate followed the poor
Queen.   The opinion was common at the time
that the fatality attending these births was a
punishment from Heaven for the illegality of
the marriage.

The Queen did not want her children to be
buried among the kings of France at Saint
Denis, for she could not then have had the
consolation of repairing frequently to weep and
pray at their tomb.   They were therefore laid to
rest in the cathedral church of Tours, and Jean
Just, a skilful artist of the school established in
that town, was commanded to erect a beautiful
monument in white marble to their memory.

Anne was much to be pitied, for, in addition
to her other sorrows, she was tortured by
jealousy caused by the infidelities of her
husband, which were carried on even before
her eyes at Amboise, where the Court had

returned after the death of the Dauphin. She lived in as much retirement as possible, and took little part in the fêtes, banquets, and pageants which were constantly going on at the Castle. About this time Charles, who was daily expected at Lyons in order again to pass the Alps, suddenly took the road to Tours under the pretext of visiting the relics of St. Martin, but in reality to follow one of the Queen's maids of honour who had been dismissed from her post in the " Cour des Dames." The Queen bore all in silence, and with tears earnestly prayed that her husband's heart might return to her. In the beginning of the year 1498, to her great joy, a remarkable change came over the King. He changed his manner of life entirely, gave up jousts and tournaments, kept away from his bad companions, and frequented the society of wise and devout men instead. Anne received him with open arms, and never allowed a word of reproach for his past faithlessness to fall from her lips. He also devoted himself with care to the internal administration of his kingdom, and determined to reform the laws and correct abuses in the secular and religious courts. Commynes says, "He gave much in alms to the poor, and a few days before his death he established a public audience, listening to everyone who had a grievance, especially to the poor. I saw him there eight days before his death for two full hours, and I never saw him again."

But the excesses of his youth were telling on his health from day to day, and he looked emaciated and dying some time before the accident occurred which hastened his death. He was preparing for a second expedition into Italy, for Savonarola, who had been instrumental in summoning him the first time, had reproached him severely for not having fulfilled his duty in reforming the Church, and prophesied that sooner or later the hand of God would weigh heavily upon him. On the morning of the fatal day, Saturday the 7th of April 1498, Charles received a letter from the holy monk of Florence summoning the King of France to Rome, and demanding the reform of the Church by the sword, at the same time threatening him with the punishment of God if

he did not accomplish this order from Heaven.
It was the eve of Palm Sunday, and Charles,
preoccupied with this message, and full of
plans for departure,—for a devout son of the
Church could not but acquiesce in what was
demanded from him,—was walking with the
Queen, his confessor, Jean de Resley, Bishop
of Angers, and some of his friends about two
o'clock in the afternoon, inspecting some work
which was being carried out in one of the courts
of the Castle at Amboise by the sculptors he
had brought back with him from Italy. The
gentlemen of his Court had that day arranged
a tennis match ; and although the King's health
no longer permitted him to take part in the
game, he had promised to go with the Queen to
see it. To reach the court where the game
was being played they had to pass through the
"Galérie Hacquelebac," so called from the name
of one of the old guards; it was the dirtiest
part of the Castle, for anyone could go to and
fro without let or hindrance. The entrance to
this gallery was so low that the King, deep in
thought, hit his head against the top of the
archway with such force that he stood for a

moment as if stunned by the violence of the blow; those around supported him, and in a few minutes he revived and went on to the tennis court to watch the game. He remained watching for some time, talking first to one and then to another, afterwards to his confessor, who was speaking to him of the Judgment of God; but while he was saying, "I sincerely hope by God's grace never more to commit sin, either mortal or venial, . . ." he fell backwards, never to rise again. A mattress was hastily fetched on which the King was laid, but the most assiduous care could not restore the dying man, who was carried into a neighbouring room, which, though mean and dirty, contained a poor bed. It was on this wretched pallet that the King of France lingered till eleven o'clock at night. The Queen, present at this sad spectacle, made dreadful moan; her cries and sobs were heard by her dying husband, but he could not speak one farewell word to her. At last it was necessary to raise her by force and take her to her room, where she mingled her tears with those of her ladies. Charles had been confessed twice that week, once on account of the approaching Easter, and again after touching several scrofulous people. Encouraged by his confessor, he received Extreme Unction, and three times he found strength to murmur, "Mon Dieu, Vierge Marie, Monseigneur Saint Claude, Monseigneur Saint Blaise me soient en aide." * He constantly made signs to show that he joined in intention with the prayers of the priests, and gave up his soul after nearly nine hours' suffering. "Thus," says Commynes, "departed from this world so great and powerful a King in so miserable a place." The blow doubtless hastened his death, but the attack of apoplexy following had been foreseen by his doctors, who had warned him only a short time before, that he might be prepared to some extent. The King, however, would only listen to a quack who assured him to the contrary, and paid no heed to what the others said. A celebrated Italian physiognomist, who saw a portrait of Charles painted from life, said, "That great King will live but a short time, and will die in a fit." He had not completed his twenty-eighth year. The arch

* Commynes.

against which Charles VIII. struck his forehead still exists at the end of the terrace at the Castle of Amboise. On it has since been carved the device of Louis XII.,—the porcupine, —and the ground beneath has been lowered.

The instant Charles had breathed his last everyone quitted his body, and, leaving him in the place where he died, galloped post-haste to Blois to announce to the Duc d'Orleans his accession to the throne. Louis was greatly shocked, and, moved to tears, he spake many things in praise of the late King in presence of the courtiers crowding round him. Towards morning Monseigneur du Bouchage arrived at Blois and gave a full account of the sad event which had just occurred. Soon afterwards the King set out for Amboise, where, on his arrival, he found the Castle in a state of desolation which rent his heart. His first visit was to the room where the late King lay, and, making a deep reverence as he entered, he sprinkled the body with holy water. Those present said there were large tears in his eyes, and he said aloud, "God will pardon him." Then he went to change his clothes after the journey and before seeing the Queen. He found her overcome with grief, and at sight of him she redoubled her sobs, saying that she wanted to join her husband. He tried to comfort her by reminding her of their old friendship, and did all in his power in the most winning way to distract her from her sorrow. When she became calmer she begged him to see that the obsequies of Charles VIII. were carried out with all the customary pomp, and told him of her intention to wear black—the symbol of constancy in love—instead of white, which was usually worn by widowed queens of France. Louis XII. gave orders that the wishes of the young widow should be fulfilled, and never were funeral ceremonies of a king of France carried out with greater magnificence. He stayed the whole of that day at Amboise, in order to make the necessary arrangements, and then returned to Blois. From his patrimony as Monseigneur d'Orleans he defrayed the whole cost of the funeral, not only of the ceremony itself, but of that incurred in conducting the body from Amboise to Saint Denis.

ANNE OF BRITTANY.
(Musée de Cluny.)

A Twice Crowned Queen

Anne's grief was so intense that for some days fears for her life were entertained; she took no nourishment for twenty-four hours, and could get no relief by sleep. To those who begged her to take care of her life, she still replied, "Je dois suivre le chemin de mon mari." This poor young Queen — not yet twenty-one years old—had already known the grief of losing mother, father, sister, and four little children, and now within a few hours the husband she loved was taken from her. For two days she remained shut up in her room lying on the floor and wringing her hands in despair. Louis, much concerned, sent to her Cardinal Briçonnet and Jean de Lamarre, Bishop of Condon, who both had much influence over the Queen. When she saw Cardinal Briçonnet, to whom the late King had been much attached, she burst into sobs and cries, and threw herself into his arms. The Cardinal tried to comfort her with words from the Gospel, but as the Queen then wept more freely, he could not restrain his own emotion, and burst into tears at the remembrance of his kind master; Jean de Lamarre, less moved,

F

then tried to calm the young wife's despair by eloquent exhortations on life and death, begging her to talk of the dead, to praise his heroic deeds, his gentle disposition, and the greatness of his courage ; at last, sustained and consoled by religion, she consented to take some nourishment, after which, as d'Argentré naïvely puts it, " Blood returned to her, and feeling better, she took comfort." *

Immediately afterwards she found strength to write to Jeanne de Laval, the good Queen of Sicily, widow of René of Anjou, to inform her of her misfortune, and signed a decree to re-establish the Chancellorship of the Duchy of Brittany.

The Sieur du Bouchage, one of the King's councillors, writes thus to his wife :

" The body of the late King, whom may God absolve, will not leave here until Monday or Tuesday. . . . The Queen weeps incessantly, and cannot be appeased. I think the King will come and see her some day this week. I hope, by the will of God, to come to you soon after the King is crowned ; do the best you can

* *Histoire de Bretagne.*

in all our affairs. I can write no more, except that I pray God, my wife, 'ma mie,' to give you all you desire, so that you may be lacking in nothing.

"Written at Amboise the 11th day of April, by the hand of your good and loyal husband,
"IMBERT DE BATARNAY."

On the 28th of April the Queen ordered two of her faithful servants, Lope de Dicastello, master of the household, and Pierre Morin, her treasurer, to arrange for the expenses of the mourning. The sum of £20,000 was fixed for the clothing of the Queen, her ladies, and servants. From her private income she ordered a considerable quantity of black cloth in silk and wool to be distributed among the princes and princesses of her family, and the lords and barons of Brittany.

Charles VIII. has been judged in many different ways by the historians of his time, some representing him as being completely without any gifts of nature or of mind, others as courageous and full of nobility and goodness. Two men of keen intellect have vilified his character—Guicciardini, always an implacable enemy of the French, and Philippe de Commynes, who could never forget the hard captivity he had undergone for participating in the revolt against Anne de Beaujeu. The accounts given by them are so obviously prompted by malice that they must be taken with some reserve. Nevertheless, it is well known that Charles was weak, obstinate, self-willed, and licentious, though, during the last few months before his death, he repented deeply that he had led so frivolous a life. Courageous no doubt he was, in spite of his delicate constitution, spurred on to emulate valiant deeds by the stories of chivalry on which he had been fed from childhood. He was eager for glory, but with an impetuous rather than a resolute will; generous but without discrimination, firm in his resolutions though rather through obstinacy than constancy. Of his goodness of heart there can be no doubt, for even Commynes says, "The said King was never anything but a puny man with very little sense, but he was so good it was impossible to behold a better creature."

Indeed, had he been so thoroughly unattractive as these historians make out, we can scarcely understand Anne, as a young girl, being so ready to break her faith with Maximilian in order to marry the French King, and still less can we understand the deplorable state of grief she was in at his death. Wraxall, in his *Memoirs of the Kings of France*, says, " Perhaps her mortified ambition may in some degree have caused such immoderate distress, as by Charles' death she found herself again reduced from Queen of France to Duchess of Brittany."

At anyrate Charles was named by his people the Affable or Courteous, and it is not known that in his whole life he ever offended or disgusted any one of his servants or subjects. Two of his servants are said to have died of grief for the loss of so beloved a master.

Zacharie Contarini, the Venetian Ambassador, gives the following account of the young King and Queen :—

" The King of France is twenty-two years of age, with a small and ill-formed person ; he has an ugly face, with large light eyes, with which he sees rather badly than well, an aquiline nose much out of proportion to the rest of his face; his lips also are big, and he keeps them constantly open; he has certain nervous movements in his hands which are not pleasant to see, and he is slow of speech. According to my opinion, which may very well be wrong, I feel convinced that in body as well as in mind he is not worth much. However, everyone in Paris praises him for his very great skill in tennis, hunting, and jousting, exercises to which for good or ill he devotes much of his time. They praise him also because he has given over the charge and government of his affairs to certain members of the secret council, and will no longer leave to others the task of deliberating. They say that in his decisions he gives proof of high intelligence. The Queen is seventeen. She also is small and thin in person, visibly lame in one foot, although she uses a false heel; very determined for her age, so much so, that if a wish enters her head, by smiles or tears, at any cost she will obtain it."

CHAPTER IV

A WEEK after the death of her husband, Anne
of Brittany, notwithstanding her deep grief,
found strength to face bravely her new position.
Such a sorrow would have deepened the most
frivolous nature, therefore it must have brought
most serious reflections to the mind of the
young widowed Queen, whose moral sense and
precocious intelligence were remarkable. Her
position, though changed and difficult in many
respects, was still a fine one, holding as she
did very high rank among the sovereigns of
Europe. Though she had lost the crown of
France, she re-entered with full power into
possession of her Duchy of Brittany, in the

A Twice Crowned Queen

government of which she had had little share during the seven years of her life with Charles VIII. Devoted as she was to her native land, the thought of returning must have been of great solace to her, seeing that she now had absolute power, and could rule without interference with her actions.

Three days after the King's death, Anne sent for Jean de Châlons, Prince of Orange, whom she entrusted with the government of Brittany for the time being.

She stayed quietly at Amboise until about the middle of May, when, in order to follow the custom observed at that time by queens-dowager of France, which obliged them to live a certain time in Paris after their widowhood, she left for the Capital and took up her abode in a house called the Hôtel d'Etampes, which was situated on the Quai Saint Paul, now Quai des Celestins, not far from the house belonging to the Archbishops of Sens. It had been built by Charles V., when Dauphin, on the site of one previously inhabited by Louis Comte d'Etampes. It was a huge building, intended for great entertainments, and when

A Twice Crowned Queen

Charles became king it remained an appanage of the Crown. This dwelling, which had on many previous occasions been relegated to the use of widowed queens, was rapidly put into a state to receive Anne of Brittany, 26,320 francs being spent on alterations and improvements. Every day the young widow wrote many letters to relations, friends, and councillors in Brittany to summon them to her side that she might receive consolation or advice. She devoted herself to the government of her Duchy, and one of her first actions was to send to the Master of the Mint at Nantes, asking him for gold and silver coin impressed with her own or her father's effigy. She summoned the principal nobles, among them the Sires de Rohan, de Rieux, d'Aigremont, and her natural brother the Baron d'Avaugour, to entrust them with the charge of the most important towns ; and to the Seigneur de Bourbon, the Prince d'Orange, and the Maréchal de Gié, begging them loyally to defend her interests. Her energy during this short stay in Paris was remarkable ; numberless letters were written, and couriers and pages sent in all directions with messages.

A Twice Crowned Queen

On the 15th of May, probably soon after her arrival, Anne received the new King Louis XII., surrounded by lords of her Duchy, and there is no doubt that after this formal visit frequent interviews took place between them. Louis had scrupulously carried out the conditions imposed on him by the late King; his armed men had left Brittany; his captains and archers in every town had been ordered to give up their charge to Breton captains and their men. Many of them, however, had refused to obey, and at Brest and St. Malo there was some disturbance. Anne, being informed of this, at once wrote to the King, and sent the Prince d'Orange to complain of this serious infraction of the promise given her. Louis hastened to satisfy her request, and punished his disobedient soldiers. In fact, he sought to please her by every means in his power, and we may judge of his success by the following significative letter written about this time :—

"MONSIEUR MON BON FRÈRE,—J'ai reçu par M. de la Pommeraye vos lettres, et avec sa charge entendu la singulière bénévolence que me portez, dont je suis très consolée; et vous en remercie de tout mon cœur, vous priant de toujours ainsi continuer, comme c'est la ferme confiance de celle qui est, et à toujours sera vôtre bonne sœur, cousine et alliée,   ANNE."

As time went on meetings between the King and the widowed Queen became more frequent ; and one cannot be surprised at the result, for Louis was as good as he was courteous and noble, and Anne fell truly and deeply in love. In June the Duchess journeyed to Etampes where the King then was, and from two acts dated on the same day, the 19th of August 1498 following, we may gather the nature of some at least of the conferences.   According to the first, Anne consents to marry Louis as soon as his compulsory union with Jeanne of France shall have been declared by the Pope to be null and void.   In the second act, Louis XII. undertakes to restore the two towns of Nantes and Fougères, which he was holding as a pledge, if, through death or any other cause, he should not marry the Duchess during the year.*   Anne had deeply regretted the loss of the crown of France, but to her great satisfac-

[1] Dom Morice, *Actes de Bretagne.*

tion she is now not only assured of the independence of Brittany, but has a good hope of again sharing the throne. The young Duchess and her councillors were singularly favoured by circumstances. It was important that they should obtain the strict fulfilment of the conditions laid down in the marriage contract with Charles VIII. These conditions obliged the new King to marry Anne of Brittany, or to unite her to the heir to the crown. Now Louis was already married, and the heir presumptive, François d'Angoulême, was only four years old; Anne, therefore, considered herself free with respect to France according to the Treaty of Nantes, and acted as Sovereign of the Duchy of Brittany. She was aware, however, that Louis Duc d'Orleans had been forced into a marriage with the daughter of Louis XI., and that he had never been able to conquer his dislike for her; that, moreover, he had expressed admiration for herself which was rapidly changing into love. Such was the state of mind of the Queen-Duchess when, replying to those who pitied her lot, she said that she would rather remain a widow all her life than marry anyone of lower rank after having been the wife of so great a king. Brantôme, who tells us this, adds that she also said : " I have enough confidence in my star to believe that I shall become for a second time Queen of France."

With her heart full of new hopes Anne left Paris about the middle of August for her beloved Brittany. She knew that Louis was already in communication with the Court of Rome with a view to disannulling his marriage, and still more that he could not fail to succeed.

Every care had been taken that her return to Brittany should be accompanied with the magnificence due to a sovereign princess. On the 13th of August she wrote to the Seigneur Coupcoul, a member of her Privy Council and Secretary of War, to send a hundred of the best archers of the Duchy to serve as her escort. On the 16th she was at Etampes, where she saw the King, and on the 24th at Chartres. She wrote to the clergy, barons, and citizens of the dioceses of Rennes, St. Malo, St. Brieuc, and Tréguier to summon them to Rennes to assist at the assembly of the Estates which she was going to hold there. Towards the end of August she arrived at Laval, where she stayed some time with the Queen-dowager of Sicily, her cousin and the godmother of the poor little Dauphin, Charles-Orland. During this visit Anne wrote many letters to the King, the Prince d'Orange, and Françoise de Dinan, her former governess, as well as to many great nobles of Brittany. It was not until October that she left for Nantes and Rennes, where she continued to occupy herself with the administration of her Duchy. She made a State entry into Nantes, and was received at the Gate of the Sauvetout bridge under a dais of black velvet, preceded by banners of white satin embroidered with her arms and device, and followed by black crosses and banners as a sign of mourning. She then repaired to the cathedral, where the Bishop, in the name of Brittany, presented her with an address of condolence.

The young Duchess commemorated her return to her dominions by many deeds of benevolence, giving alms and presenting rich gifts to the churches.

A Twice Crowned Queen

While at Nantes she experienced fresh grief at the loss of Françoise de Dinan, for whom she had always shown great affection.

Anne established her private household on a new footing, and increased the number and wages of those who composed it ; and from this time dates the formation of a company of a hundred Breton gentlemen, whose office it was to guard her person and to accompany her on her journeys.

Whilst Anne, rejoicing in the complete possession of her Duchy, was exercising all her rights as a sovereign princess, Louis XII., who for many months had been urging at the Court of Rome the dissolution of his marriage with Jeanne, at last obtained on this point all that he desired.

Louis XII. was great-grandson of Charles V., and son of Charles Duc d'Orleans who was taken prisoner at Agincourt when eighteen years of age. Saint Gelais, the chronicler, says, that on his return to France, at Blois and every town through which he passed, the people rejoiced as though an angel had descended from heaven.

A Twice Crowned Queen

Louis' mother was Mary of Cleves, niece of the Duke of Burgundy, who brought up the boy wisely and well. At the age of sixteen he was the best jumper, wrestler, and tennis player that could be found in France; he was an expert archer, a skilful man of arms, and the best rider and trainer of horses ever seen. "And I have good cause to know it," says the chronicler, "for I have seen him ride the wildest horse, and tame it more successfully than anyone, and armed for war and joust his equal was not to be found . . . and it is also to be noted that in all the games and pastimes of youth he was the gentlest, the kindest, and the most gracious, and there was no one who so much feared to do anything to displease or annoy any poor gentleman whatsoever, and to tell the truth, all that he did was pleasant and agreeable to all, and showed that he was descended from very good and virtuous princes. And, in respect of his lady mother, there was not a better, sweeter, kinder, more charitable woman in the world, nor one who more nobly carried out works of mercy in her lifetime."

The marriage of Louis Duc d'Orleans with

A Twice Crowned Queen

Jeanne de France had been brought about against his will and under the terrible pressure of Louis XI., who, it was well known, would not scruple to make use of any means whatever in order to accomplish his designs. Jeanne was but ill-favoured by nature; her face was dark and plain, her figure short and deformed. Her father looked upon her with such aversion that her tutor, the Seigneur de Lesguière, used to hide her in his long robe when the King met her; and if by chance he saw her he would exclaim spitefully, "I shouldn't have thought anyone could be so ugly!" Louis d'Orleans was fourteen and Jeanne twelve when the marriage was first suggested. The boy began by refusing angrily, declaring that he would rather marry the simplest damoiselle of Beauce. Louis XI. replied that unless he submitted he should receive the tonsure, and that under the monk's habit he could easily be got rid of. The young Prince at length resigned himself, but told his friends that it should be a marriage only in name.

Jeanne herself was too modest and humble of heart to be under any delusion as to her physical disadvantages, though at the same time rejoicing at an alliance of which her heart approved. One day, admiring the proud bearing of the Duc d'Orleans on horseback, she said with a sigh to her doctor, Salomon de Bombelles: "Ah! Maître Salomon, je n'ai pas personage pour un tel prince." Another time her tutor whispered to her, "Madame, speak to Monseigneur and show some affection for him." She replied sadly, her eyes full of tears, "I should not dare to speak to him, for you yourself and everyone can see that he pays no heed to me!"

Louis d'Orleans did not consider the accession of Charles VIII. an opportune time to seek a divorce from his wife, but he lived apart from her as much as possible. Her devotion, wit, good sense, and moral qualities did not succeed in gaining her husband's affection, and when he became King of France, two powerful motives, interest and love, led him to urge a dissolution of the marriage. State reasons demanded that he should marry the young widow of Charles VIII., and he already felt great affection and admiration for her which soon developed into passion. He was sure also of obtaining from the then reigning Pope the nullity of his first marriage. This Pope was the famous Roderigo Borgia, the rich and powerful Cardinal, who, after having been for a long time the Church's Vice-chancellor, became Pope in 1492 under the name of Alexander VI. Not a man to hesitate where his interests were concerned, he readily agreed to pronounce the desired sentence in return for certain honours and awards to be conferred on his son, Cæsar Borgia. A mock trial was held before three papal commissioners, and on the 18th of December 1498 the decree annulling the marriage was placed in the King's hands at Chinon, by Cæsar Borgia, clad in cloth of gold covered with priceless jewels and attended by a magnificent retinue. He was created Duke of Valentinois, in Dauphiné, given a pension of 20,000 gold crowns, and promised the hand of one of the King's relations.

As soon as Louis had obtained the decree of separation from Jeanne, he hastened to assure to her a position worthy of her birth and rank. The Duchy of Berri with the domains of

Châtillon-sur-Indre, Châteauneuf-sur-Loire, and Pontoise, and an income of 12,000 crowns were granted to her as dowry. The pious and gentle Princess profited by these temporal riches to do all sorts of good works ; she retired to the town of Bourges, and founded the religious order of the Annonciade, of which she became Superior.

Louis' next step was to demand from Anne of Brittany the fulfilment of the agreement they had made a few months before. Anne willingly acceded to his desire, and a few days before the end of the ninth month of her widowhood, she repaired to Nantes, where the King of France had just arrived. He was not like Charles VIII., a conqueror with real rights to the succession of the Duchy, who, to stop further bloodshed, consented to marry a young girl who had fallen into his power, but a King who came to woo a reigning Duchess, because not only his interest but his heart was concerned. This was well known to Anne's prudent counsellors, and they willingly prepared the marriage contract. By this deed, Anne not only stipulated for the government of her Duchy and the exclusive use of its revenue, but should she die without children, the Duchy was to revert to her direct heirs "sans que les autres rois ses successeurs en pussent quereller." In the event of children being born, the second male child or daughter, in default of a son, should be the rightful heir to the Duchy. Anne was to enjoy, during her life, the dowry which had been assigned to her by Charles VIII., moreover the amount was doubled by Louis, and a few days later, on the 19th of January 1498, he ratified all the privileges of the Church, Courts of Justice, and other public offices in Brittany.

The marriage of Louis XII. and Anne took place in the chapel of the Castle of Nantes the following year, on 8th January 1499. To celebrate the occasion, the Queen gave magnificent presents to the churches of Brittany, and ordered the Sieur de la Bonnardière, Captain of the town and Castle of Nantes, and her treasurer Gilles Thomas, to distribute a large quantity of linen among the hospitals of her capital.

Louis remained in Brittany for most of the

winter, taking so much pleasure in hunting that, according to Saint Gelais, this pastime soon became very fashionable with the nobles, and enormous sums of money were spent by them in pursuit of it.

About the beginning of April the King and Queen journeyed to Blois, and as grand a reception as that which was given on her first marriage signalised the Queen's re-entry into France. The inhabitants of Amboise especially, eager to make the Queen forget her grief and the loss she had sustained there, celebrated with much festivity her return within their walls. The boulevard between the river Loire and the Castle was transformed into a huge pavilion, in the middle of which were erected two columns bearing the devices of Louis and Anne, a porcupine and an ermine, and from the mouth of each wine poured; a dais of red damask had been prepared for the King and one of white for the Queen; but Anne alone took part in this ceremony, either because Louis was prevented from being present, or because he did not wish, by his presence, to recall sad memories.

A Twice Crowned Queen

Blois was the birthplace of Louis XII. and always his favourite residence; he rebuilt the east front of the Castle in red brick—doubtless about this time, as it was completed in 1501. The royal pair, however, did not long enjoy retirement here, for Louis was preparing for war in Italy, and crossed the Alps in the August following his marriage. Anne, too, was soon driven away by the plague, and sought a refuge with Louise de Savoie, Duchesse d'Angoulême, at Romorantin, about thirty miles south of Blois. Here, on the 15th of October 1499, she gave birth to a daughter, Claude, destined to become Queen of France as the wife of Francis I. She was called Claude because the Queen had dedicated her to the saint of that name, usually invoked in perilous circumstances and at the approach of death. The King received the news in a town near Milan, and expressed great joy; for, said he, "There is good hope of having a son, since one has a daughter." However, this birth, at which all France was rejoicing with the King, was accompanied and followed by evil omens, which popular credulity took good care to observe. For several months continual rains had prevented the vines from ripening, the plague had broken out in Paris, and its ravage was so great that Parliament suspended all civil affairs; but to the superstition of the time the fall of the old bridge of Nôtre Dame in Paris, on the 29th October, seemed an event of ill fortune, graver than the plague.

The King's eagerness to see the Queen increased from day to day, so he left Milan at the end of November and returned to his kingdom as quickly as possible. He stayed but a short time at Lyons, where his presence caused unanimous joy, took a boat to Roanne, then mounted a horse and rode post-haste to Romorantin. Anne welcomed her husband with transports of joy, and the tender reception she gave him showed how she had wearied in his absence. A few days after the baptism of the young Princess, the King and his wife returned to Blois, taking with them the little Princess,—already called Madame,—who spent the first years of her life in this town. Although very puny, it was several years before she had a serious illness, and she was always the best loved by her mother, who bestowed on her the most tender care and affection. Her solicitude was the greater because she had lost all confidence in doctors, and accused them of ignorance and frivolity for not warning her in time of the danger the little Dauphin, Charles-Orland, was running. When about eight months old the little Claude was entrusted to the care of Madame du Bouchage, for Anne wished to fulfil the vow she had made at the celebrated Abbey of Sainte Claude in Franche-Comté. From there she went on to Lons-le-Saunier in Burgundy to do honour to the Prince d'Orange, by being godmother to his son. The baptism was celebrated by banquets, dances, and joyous pastimes, which the Queen adorned by "the grace of her person."

On her return from Burgundy, the Queen gave orders for a tournament to take place at Lyons, to which place she had gone in order to meet her husband; the day fixed was the 22nd of May, and it was to be held before the Abbey of Ainay; seven gentlemen of her household were to measure lances with seven of the King's in honour of their respective ladies.

A Twice Crowned Queen

They entered the lists with their mistresses riding pillion behind them; these ladies then dismounted and took their places on the stand erected for the Queen and her maids of honour. The King's knights wore white cloaks and the trappings of their horses were white also; the Queen's wore blue embroidered with yellow and little wooden beads. The King sat on a separate stand with the princes and great nobles, and the tournament commenced with the sound of trumpets and drums. Many lances were broken and sword thrusts given. In the first onslaught the Infant of Navarre, struck by his adversary's lance, was thrown from his saddle, wounded in the face, and so stunned that for a long time he could not lift his head; another ardent jouster, Captain Poquedenare, himself drew out the broken piece of a lance which had been thrust into his arm, and used his sword so well that each stroke he made sent his adversary's blood flowing to the ground.

Louis XII.'s love for his wife increased day by day, and he, who in his youth had carried on many flirtations, proved himself to be the most faithful of husbands. He did not interfere with the administration of the Duchy of Brittany, and he allowed his wife a large share of independence in all her actions. To those who urged that the wishes of the Queen sometimes bordered on obstinacy, he replied: "Something must be conceded to a chaste woman!" With her first husband Anne had been timid and reserved, but now she was firm in conduct, bold and enterprising in her undertakings, and did not scruple to interfere in the gravest matters.

Many letters addressed to her uncle, Ferdinand of Spain, show her kindness of heart and determined character. One was written in favour of the Queen's natural brother, the Seigneur d'Avaugour, whom Anne was constantly loading with benefits; another treats of the bishopric of Pampeluna, with which Nicholas de Dicastillo, her grand almoner, had been invested. Ignoring this, the new Pope Pius III. had just given this bishopric to the Cardinal de Saint-Anastasie. Anne asks the King and Queen of Spain to join with her in entreating the Holy Father to grant the bishopric to Dicastillo and not to the Cardinal, "considering," says the Queen, with great good sense, "that there is only one cathedral church in Navarre, it is necessary that the bishop should always live on the spot."

Another, unfortunately incomplete, has reference to the war of 1503. Many Spanish vessels on their way to Flanders had been captured by the French fleet. Ferdinand and Isabella hastened to write to their good niece, who replied that justice should be done as the case demanded, and that Louis XII. and she herself would act towards their Majesties as towards their own parents.

Louis, in his moments of gaiety, called his wife "ma Bretonne," because of the tenacity of character she always showed. Never for an instant did Anne forget that she was born the sovereign of a country which until now had enjoyed complete independence. Foreseeing that she would not leave a male heir, she did all in her power to affiance her daughter Claude —who would have a rich dowry in the Duchy of Brittany—to Charles of Austria, afterwards Charles V. Claude of France was scarcely eighteen months old when negotiations were entered into to discuss the conditions of alliance. On the 11th of April 1501, Philippe-le-Beau Archduke of Austria sent ambassadors to Louis asking the hand of this child for Charles his son who was still a minor. In the month of August following, a contract of marriage was drawn up, in which among other things, the following words may be read : " The King and Queen with the authority pertaining to them, promise on the word of a King and Queen to do all in their power to procure that as soon as Madame Claude shall come to marriageable age, she shall take as husband and spouse Monseigneur de Luxembourg." This marriage project, menacing the Bretons with foreign domination, was received by them with silent disapprobation and sadness, but Anne herself did not disguise the satisfaction she felt at having chosen for her son-in-law the future Emperor of Germany and King of Spain. She honoured the ambassadors of the Archduke in a special manner, and invited them to a banquet followed by a masquerade in which French, Spanish, German, Lombard, and Poitevin dances were arranged to amuse the guests. Each dancer wore a costume of the country, and these dresses of cloth of gold and silk were provided at the Queen's expense. Princes, nobles, and the most charming young ladies took part in these mummeries. During the evening, the Sire de Néry, who entered the hall dressed as a Turk and holding a bow, was repulsed in turn by all the ladies, and retired sad and dejected without having a single dance. This little diversion was intended to represent the alliance of France, Germany, Spain, and Italy against the Turk.

After this Louis went for a few days' hunting in the woods of Dauphiné, and Anne, impatient to see her daughter Claude, returned to Blois, where she had left her under the care of the Dame du Bouchage. The least delay in obtaining news of the child put the Queen in a state of anxiety, and she constantly complained of the want of letters, although Madame du Bouchage repeated by nearly every post: "Votre fille fait bonne chère et se fait bien nourrir."

Towards the end of November the Archduke Philip and his wife Joanna came to

A Twice Crowned Queen

France on a visit to Louis, and were received with much ceremony. The new and magnificent buildings of the Castle of Blois had just been finished, and great luxury was displayed on this occasion. The Queen gave orders that a large quantity of silver plate which had been left in her Castle of Nantes should be brought to Blois; but first it was made to look as good as new, and her arms were engraved upon it. Details of the ceremonies which took place on this occasion have come down to us, and have been published by De la Saussaye in his *Histoire du Château de Blois.* The Queen-Duchess, seated on a throne, received the Archduchess, then rose, took two steps forward and embraced her. Little Claude was to take part in the ceremony, but she began to cry so loudly when she saw the Austrian Princess that it was impossible to say "Dieu gard" to her or show her any attention, and Madame de Tournon was obliged to carry her back to her room.

For many years Louis cherished the same ideas as his wife with regard to the House of Austria, since by letters of the 22nd of

A Twice Crowned Queen

September 1504 he grants to Charles of Luxembourg the monopoly of a tax levied in Artois in favour of his marriage with Claude of France. It was not until 1506, after the serious illness which placed his life in danger, that he changed his opinion and yielded to the urgent entreaties of his favourite Minister, Georges d'Amboise, who put before him all the dangers of an alliance with Austria, and became the interpreter of a wish formed not only in Brittany, but throughout the whole of France, that the Princess Claude should marry the heir to the throne, François d'Angoulême.

CHAPTER V

ANNE ever took great interest in Louis' various
Italian expeditions, although in her heart she
questioned the wisdom of them. Begun in
1499 by the conquest of the Milanese in twenty
days, they ended, after twelve years of mingled
success and defeat, in the complete evacuation
of Italy by the French. Louis, on ascending
the throne, had assumed the titles of Duke of
Milan and King of Naples, thus announcing
his intention of asserting his claim to the Duchy
of Milan through his grandmother, Valentina
Visconti, and to the Kingdom of Naples
through the House of Anjou. In 1501 he

H   113

determined, with the help of the King of Spain, Ferdinand the Catholic, to make a combined attack on the kingdom of Naples, and to take possession by force of arms, in order to divide it between them. In pursuance of this design, the French army under Stuart d'Aubigny, and that of Spain under the great Captain, Gonsalvo of Cordova, marched to Rome without meeting with any opposition, and the Pope was induced to concur in the iniquitous scheme of depriving Ferdinand of Naples of his throne. This monarch, finding the position hopeless, resigned himself to his fate, and having given up his capital and all his fortresses, Louis conferred on him the Province of Maine, and permitted him and his family to retire there with a pension of 30,000 livres a year. The unfortunate monarch only lived for three years after his dethronement, and died at Tours in 1504. This wicked spoliation of a kingdom did not bring any good to France; quarrels arose between the two monarchs when the division of territory had to be settled, and, unable to come to any agreement, hostilities broke out in the summer of 1502 between the two armies, and in 1503 Gonsalvo gained two decisive victories over the French, and took entire possession of Naples—only a few small towns and the fortresses of Venosa and Gaeta remaining in the hands of the French. Louis, though astounded at the course of these events, did not lose heart, but quickly raised three new armies, one of which was destined to invade Spain, another to attack Roussillon, while the third, under the command of the veteran general La Trémouille, was to cross the Alps and join the scattered remains of d'Aubigny's army. Delay in the march, however, occurred in Rome owing to the death of Pope Alexander VI., and when at last the French marched southwards, La Trémouille was attacked by fever and had to resign his command to the Marquis of Mantua, a brave soldier but an indifferent general, who so ill managed the expedition, that on the 27th of September 1503 he was attacked on the banks of the Garigliano by Gonsalvo at so great a disadvantage that this fatal battle is memorable as being one of the most disastrous that ever befell the French, and very few of the gallant soldiers ever saw their native land again. This complete rout, and the ignominious peace he was forced to make, greatly distressed Louis, who felt it so acutely that it brought on an alarming illness to which he nearly succumbed.

While these untoward events were taking place in Italy, the Queen had come triumphantly out of a struggle in which she had been engaged against François de Rohan, Maréchal de Gié, favourite Minister of Louis. It is but just to say that this is not a fine page of her history, but Anne's enemies have perhaps exaggerated her conduct through inadequate knowledge of the circumstances. In 1503, when Louis, struck to the heart by the double defeat of his army in Italy, fell seriously ill, there were two distinct parties at the Court, and these were in perpetual strife. One was the Queen's party, composed of the Breton lords who had remained faithful to their country, and a few French, among them the Admiral de Graville, an old favourite of Charles VIII., who had fallen into disgrace for disapproving of the Italian expeditions; the other was Louise de Savoie's party, at the

head of which was Pierre de Rohan, Maréchal
de Gié, formerly tutor to the young prince, and
a disdained suitor for the hand of Louise de
Savoie, who, though still young, had remained
a widow. In 1503, when the doctors declared
that Louis' death was imminent, the Maréchal
de Gié sent to inform Louise de Savoie, and
ordered Louis de Montroyal, who now filled
his place, on no account to leave the young
Prince, François d'Angoulême; he caused the
banks of the Loire to be guarded by 10,000
archers, so that Madame Claude could not be
carried off, and then returned to Amboise
to watch over the doings of the Queen.*
Anne of Brittany, mindful of all the difficulties awaiting her on the death of Louis
XII., ordered the officers of her household
to load two or three big boats with her
belongings, plate, furniture, etc., and to
send them by the Loire to Nantes. The
Maréchal de Gié stopped these boats on their
way, saying, with reason, that Louis XII. still
lived and that the Queen therefore had no
right to act thus. Anne's two marriage

* *Chroniques de Jean d'Auton.*

contracts guaranteed her the possession of her furniture, so in acting thus she would have been justified had the King indeed been dead. Moreover, she looked upon the Maréchal as the irreconcilable enemy of her House, for he was the first among the Breton princes to give himself and his intellect to the service of France, and had always thwarted her in the design she had cherished since her marriage with Louis, of leaving Brittany independent after her death. At her command he was arrested and put in prison; a charge of peculation and high treason was brought against him, and he was dragged from place to place to be confronted with accusers whom the old favourite would not expect to meet. Even Louise de Savoie, for once in agreement with the Queen, came to an inn at Amboise to bring some futile accusations against her son's late tutor. The Maréchal only said, "If I had served God as I have served you, Madame, I should not have a big account to render Him."

When Louis was thought to be dying, the Maréchal wrote to the Sire Alain d'Albret to tell him to have the 10,000 men under his

command in readiness to ensure the safety of
the Kingdom. They found matter for accusa-
tion in this order, and d'Albret, a fierce enemy
of de Gié because he had been conquered in
the efforts they both made to obtain the hand
of Marguerite d'Armagnac, heiress of Nemours,
was only too glad to join in crushing his
rival. De Gié was brought before him in his
Castle of Dreux, and d'Albret received him
lying on his bed playing with a little monkey.
The accused was told to sit on a mean bench,
and the monkey springing upon him fiercely
seized his long beard. De Gié angrily laid
hold of the mischievous animal and flung it
to the ground. The ape got up, says Jean
d'Auton, jumped back to his master's bed and
made grimaces at the poor Maréchal. This
unseemly incident sent d'Albret and the lords
of Council into fits of laughter. With such
unworthy judges there was little hope for the
accused ; a verdict was drawn up against him ;
he was condemned to be beheaded, his goods
were to be confiscated, and his children declared
incapable of succeeding, because their father
was guilty of high treason. This was going

too far; Louis XII. could not allow such injustice. The trial was referred to the Parliament of Toulouse, which was ordered to modify the decision of the original judges. The Maréchal was only suspended from office for five years, deprived of his men-at-arms, compelled to remain ten leagues distant from any place where the Court might be, and obliged to restore the money to those he had employed on the works of his Castle of Fronsac. The fallen favourite retired to his estate called " Le Verger " in Anjou, where he had built a splendid mansion at immense cost. He bore his disgrace with dignity, and as he was still young he said, with reason, that " the rain had fallen early."

Louis proposed to spend the winter of 1503–1504 in Paris, and to this Anne willingly consented, delighted at the prospect of showing herself there a second time as Queen. Immense preparations were made for her reception and for being crowned a second time. The King wrote from Fontainebleau to Paris to announce that his " very dear and well-beloved consort wished to make her entry," and to inform the citizens that he desired she should be received "joyously and honourably, in every way as he himself would be."

On the 18th of November, Anne went to receive the crown from the hands of the Cardinal Legate in the Abbey of Saint Denis; the next day she slept at the village of La Chapelle. About noon she entered her litter and arrived at Paris by the gate of Saint Denis, above which was erected a huge heart representing Paris, and supported by Justice, the clergy, and the people. Within the heart were two fair girls, personifying Loyalty and Honour, who were presented to the Queen with complimentary verses. Sacred mysteries were represented in various places, and at the Porte aux Peintres a scaffold was erected on which stood the five Annes of Holy Scripture, and verses were recited, in which to these five praiseworthy ladies a sixth was added, "Anne the noble Queen of France, who preserves her people from want." Many of these mysteries were given at the expense of the merchant guilds, and produced by those who usually undertook such work, Pierre Gringoire writing

121

the verses and Jean Marchand arranging the decorations and costumes. Surrounded by the nobility of Brittany and France, Anne was conducted, under the canopy of the six trade guilds, to Nôtre Dame, through streets hung with rich tapestry ; but though the actors in the mysteries praised the excellence of the ermine, which they associated with the magnificence of the lily, the cold and critical welcome she received from the people showed that they always saw the Duchess of Brittany in the Queen of France. She knew well that discontented faces and hostile jests awaited the entry which she had postponed for six years. At the end of the day a splendid supper was given in the great hall of the Palais ; the Queen sat in the middle of the marble table, and below her the gentlemen of the Court, town dignitaries, and members of Parliament. This supper, to which more than a thousand guests had been invited, doubtless displayed all the marvels of the "cuisine épicée et aromatisée" which the celebrated Taillevent, Charles v.'s cook, had taught in his *Viandier*, one of the first books printed in France, a "very useful and profitable book to dress meats and serve banquets."

The fêtes attending the entry were to continue until the end of December ; a tournament was to be given in Anne's honour, and the students of the Basoche had obtained permission to perform a morality play before the Queen and the King, who was to arrive on the 26th of December for the parliamentary session. He wished to patronise the drama, and especially the revival of the satirical comedies of Aristophanes. "I want them to act in freedom," he said to La Trémouille, alluding to the farces of Gringoire and Jean Bouchet, "I want the young people to expose the abuses of my Court, since the confessors and those who profess to be wise don't like saying anything about them. Provided always that they do not speak of my wife, for I wish the honour of the ladies to be safeguarded."

The tournament was held in the courtyard of the Hôtel de Nesle, that Gothic mansion whose big tower recalls the crimes of Jeanne de Bourgogne, whose lovers of the night before were thrown into the river in the morning.

A Twice Crowned Queen

This virtuous Queen Anne, who patronised chivalry and was to reward the conqueror in the jousts, bore herself the more proudly since her enemy Pierre de Rohan was not at hand to thwart her.

The feats of arms were brilliant, and the victory was gallantly disputed by gentlemen who had assembled from the farthest provinces, and even from foreign countries. A terrible accident, not unusual in these dangerous games, interrupted them but for a moment. François de Maugiron, one of the King's two hundred gentlemen-at-arms, was matched against Supplanville, "très gentil et plein de cœur"; they attacked each other so violently that Maugiron's lance pierced his adversary's cuirass and went right through his body, so that he fell in a pool of blood. After this dreadful episode and many more feats of arms which effaced it, the students of the Basoche held their performance.

They satirised the faults of the Court, town, army, and clergy, the feuds of the nobility, and the extortions of the treasurers. The death of the Borgia Pope, Alexander vi., and the efforts made by the Cardinal Legate, Georges d'Amboise, to succeed him, served as texts for bitter mockeries, and excited the gaiety of the audience, but could not fail to wound the susceptibilities of many people present. Until now, Louis, though astonished at the boldness of the players, had laughed with the rest, but was much annoyed when the intrigues of the Dominicans, Jean Clérée and Pierre Dufour, to replace his confessor, Laurent Bureau, who had died at Blois a short time before, were thus made public. Anne very soon shared the King's anger, for these impertinent "baso-chiens" took it into their heads to play upon the disgrace of the Maréchal de Gié, who was then in prison during his trial. One of the actors said to Pierre de Rohan, who was represented on the scene, that, " Trop chauffer cuit, trop parler nuit," in allusion to his excess of zeal. In another piece the satire was still more direct, one of the players saying, "Il y avait un Maréchal qui avait voulu ferrer une Âne, mais elle lui avait donné un si grand coup de pied, qu'elle l'avait jeté hors de la cour par-dessus les murailles jusques dans le Verger."

A Twice Crowned Queen

Louis XII. forbade these farces for the future, and banished several of these over-bold students in order to give an example of fear to the others. However, the farce was played in many colleges in Paris at the same time. Anne had been publicly insulted, and, in spite of the punishment of the delinquents, she always kept their satire in bitter remembrance, perhaps attributing it to the friends and sympathisers of the poor Maréchal. Brantôme says that the Queen did not wish for the death of De Gié, and the reason he gives is a strange one. "Death," she said, "is the true remedy for all our ills and griefs, and being dead he would be too happy." She wanted him to live ruined and disparaged, which would cause him more pain a hundred times than death itself; for death would last but a day, an hour even, but the bitterness he would suffer living would cause him to die every day.

Anne was dull and "distraite" in the midst of her Court, so Jean d'Auton, historiographer to the King, wrote verses exalting the female sex, especially "the good, beautiful, generous and prudent Queen of Honour—a pattern for the good." The Queen submitted to this praise of her virtues even when her vengeance was inexorably following her enemy Pierre de Rohan, greatly to the distress of the King.

At this time the country people, especially those of the southern provinces, were suffering such misery that the towns were dismayed at their cries of distress. The drought of the preceding year had caused a famine, which was made more terrible by thoughts of the coming winter; harvest was yet far off, and much land lay fallow for want of grain to sow it. Lyons, for example, presented a deplorable spectacle; poor people, women and children from the neighbouring villages and from Savoy, wandered through the streets begging for bread; charity and fear opened the hearts of the rich citizens; all who possessed anything gave according to their ability, and those who always gave to the poor distributed more of their goods than ever; nevertheless this help was not enough to feed so many strangers who left their houses empty and their fields unsown. Sickness, caused by privation of all kinds, broke out among these unhappy

creatures, and numbers died. The King,
deeply touched by miseries which he could
do little to alleviate because his revenue was
not as great as his humanity, distributed alms
and gifts with discerning zeal, and lightened
the burden of taxation. Anne, because of
the penury of the Royal treasury and the
distress of the people, herself paid all the
expenses of the Maréchal's trial, which
amounted to 31,900 Tours pounds.

On the 4th of February 1505, Jeanne de
France, Louis' first wife, died. Since her
divorce she had lived in seclusion in her
Duchy of Berri, under the spiritual direction
of her confessor Gilbert Maria and the good
hermit François de Paule. She made it her
glory and joy to minister to the sick and poor,
and the hospitals, churches, and colleges of
Bourges shared her benefits and pious works.
During her life she was called the "bienheur-
euse Jeanne," and even Pope Alexander VI.
rendered homage to the holiness of this Princess
by granting 10,000 days indulgence to all who
should say the rosary of ten aves composed
by Jeanne in honour of the ten virtues of the

A Twice Crowned Queen

Blessed Virgin which she endeavoured to imitate: chastity, prudence, humility, faith, obedience, devotion, poverty, patience, charity, and compassion. Her devotion gradually became more contemplative and solitary. She founded and directed the order of the Annonciade, but did not consider herself worthy to accept the title of "mère ancille," so only took the habit of the nuns—the grey robe, symbol of repentance, the white cloak, of purity, and the red scapulary, of the blood of Christ. Her health became much impaired by the painful penances she underwent, and her soul was continually aspiring towards heaven. On the night of the 4th of February she breathed her last sigh without a single regret at leaving the things of this world, and a heavenly light appeared around her as a reflection from Paradise. Her body was found covered with a hair shirt, iron chains, and bruises. She was buried in her convent of the Annonciade, as she had given orders in her will; her tomb attracted pilgrims, and there miracles were performed until 1562, when the Huguenots burnt her relics but were unable to destroy the remembrance of her edifying and charitable life. Her marriage with Louis was so much forgotten that her name was placed in the litanies of the Virgin. She herself seemed to have wished this, for she often had herself painted in her books of Hours, and on stained glass windows, as kneeling at the feet of the Infant Jesus, who presents her with a ring and takes her as a celestial spouse. Jeanne's death was much deplored by the inhabitants of Bourges, especially by the poor; but the King, devout as he was toward the memory of the dead, did not grant a funeral service to the Duchesse de Berri, apparently not wishing to show remorse or regret. Jean d'Auton does not even record this event in his Chronicle. It was received with indifference by the Court, at anyrate in the Queen's presence.

The King, having spent three months in Paris, became ill again, and the doctors ordered change of air, attributing the impaired state of his health to the cold and damp of the Capital during the winter, which had been a rainy one. The King felt very weak and anxious; but remembering that he had before been cured by breathing his native air, left for Blois accompanied by the Queen. The journey was delayed until the body of his father, Duke Charles, had been transferred from the Church of Saint Sauveur at Blois to that of the Célestins at Paris, the burying - place of his family. Soon after his arrival at Blois he felt much better, the fever abated and his strength returned, but he abused his convalescence by making "trop bonne chère," and became ill again soon after Easter. The Queen, "who loved him as herself," was at her post night and day to serve him, and never left his room. All around were deeply grieved, but hid their tears. Anne herself endeavoured to look cheerful though she knew the King to be in danger of death, and before him showed a smiling face and addressed him with "joyeuses paroles." At times her courage failed her, and she then wept and sobbed so much that the good chronicler says, "It was an admirable thing to see her grief." The desperate state of the King was soon known throughout the country, and a universal cry of grief arose from one end of France to the other. In Italy, too, the sad news spread rapidly. Every heart felt regret and anxiety; prayers, Masses, and processions succeeded one another in all the parishes of France, and clergy, nobles, and people implored God to grant that their good Prince might recover. At Blois, Amboise, and Tours men and women went naked into the churches and were scourged in order to interest Heaven in restoring health to him they were in so great fear of losing. On all sides were sad and grief-stricken faces; everywhere chanting and prayers, candles burning, relics exposed to the faithful, and bells ringing. Anne, whose heart was "infiniment donné" to her country of Brittany, and who would not have stayed a day in France after her husband's death, awaited with increasing anxiety the dreaded moment. Her bodyguard, composed of a hundred devoted men, most of them belonging to the old nobility of Brittany, waited night and day on the "Perche des Bretons"—the terrace adjoining her apartments. Many times the doctors and those round the King's bedside thought his soul had passed away; the rumour spread before it could be contradicted, and public desolation was so great, it seemed as though each had lost his nearest and dearest. Preparations were even being made for the funeral when the King rallied and continued to improve. No one doubted but that he had been miraculously preserved by his own merits and the prayers of the people.

Louis was barely restored to health when, with his consent, the Queen left him to visit Brittany, and to fulfil her vow at Nôtre Dame de Folgoët. During the King's illness, each person round the patient had dedicated him to his own special saint, La Trémouille to Nôtre Dame di Liesse, for instance, and the people of Paris to Sainte Geneviève, whose shrine, according to the then prevailing custom, was carried round the town in public calamities. The Queen, however, had dedicated her husband to the Breton Virgin of Folgoët, and made a vow, that if he recovered she would make a pilgrimage there during the year. With joy, therefore, she hastened to fulfil it, for she was thus able to pay a visit of several months to her Duchy of Brittany. It was a veritable triumph; many princes and French nobles accompanied her, and the Bretons eagerly joined the procession. "All the towns through which she passed were hung with rich cloths," says Jean d'Auton, "and the roads were made clean." The clergy and country gentlemen, merchants and all the people, went to meet her, and welcomed her with hearty goodwill and joyous feasting. At Nantes and at Rennes she remained about five months, held her States' Assembly, and put all the affairs of her country in order. Albert le Grand, in his *History of the Saints of Brittany*, speaks of this journey which the Queen-Duchess made in 1505 : "Her Majesty arrived at Nôtre Dame de Folgoët on Tuesday the 19th of August, established a sacristan to care for the ornaments, three choir children to help in the music, had the dome of the church completed, and did many other good works there." The same author adds, that from Nôtre Dame de Folgoët she went to Les Neven, Saint Pol, and Morlaix, where she was received with great magnificence. A tree of Jesse, set up in the cemetery of the Convent of Saint Dominique, where she lodged, was much admired. It set forth her genealogy from Conan Meriadec. At the top was a young girl representing Her Majesty, who made a fine speech. The town offered the Queen a little gold ship enriched with precious stones, and a tame ermine, white as snow, wearing round its neck a collar of stones of great price. This little animal sprang into the Queen's arms, on to her breast, which much alarmed her; but the Seigneur de Rohan, who was near her, said, "Madame, what do you fear? It is your own emblem."

While at Morlaix, Anne's left eye became inflamed, and caused her much suffering. She thought of the miracle-working finger of St. John preserved at Plougaznou, near Morlaix, in the diocese of Tréguier, in a little church called St. Janarbis, or St. Jean-du-doigt, and wrote to the canons, rectors of Plougaznou, to bring her without delay the finger of the holy Apostle. The rectors of Plougaznou and of the neighbourhood assembled solemnly in the church and placed the relic on a rich litter, which they carried themselves on their shoulders. Scarcely had they crossed the cemetery belonging to the church when the litter broke. They had to stop to put it right again, but the holy relic had disappeared. After a great search accompanied by fervent prayers, they found it in a cupboard in its accustomed place. Albert le Grand, who tells the story of this miracle, adds that the messengers of the Queen hastened back to Morlaix to report the occurrence. Anne recognised the fault she had committed, and knelt to ask pardon. She wished, as a penance, to go on foot from Morlaix to Plougaznou, but eventually agreed to be carried in a litter as far as a spot of waste land called Lann Festour, near the church, and went the rest of the way on foot, followed by prelates, princes, and the lords of her household. The next day at the hour of matins, after the Queen had finished her devotions and received the communion, the Bishop of Nantes took the holy relic, showed it to those assembled, and applied it to the Queen's eye. She presented to the church a large chalice of silver-gilt in which to place the crystal enshrining the relic, and silver candlesticks and censers engraved with the arms of

A Twice Crowned Queen

France and Brittany, and contributed a sum of money annually to help in maintaining the building and services.

Madame Claude remained at Blois with her father, and every day news of the King was sent to Anne. His health still gave much anxiety to the doctors, because his illness had left him so weak and suffering, but after a time his strength had sufficiently returned to enable him to visit his heir, who was being brought up at the Castle of Amboise with his sister Marguerite. Francis, made Duc de Valois in 1499, was eager for pleasure, impetuous and boisterous in his games, a lover of luxury, generous to a fault, careless of danger, greedy for glory, and fitted for all exercises both of the body and the mind. Many young nobles of about his own age were the companions of his studies and sports. Among them were four of whom he was particularly fond : Montmorency, Monchenu, Brion, and Robert de la Marck, who called himself "le jeune aventureux" in imitation of the Knights of the Round Table. L'Aventureux, who had been fed from babyhood on histories of old chivalrous deeds, related them to his young friends, and they, inflamed with emulation, thought only of fine actions which should surpass those of Amadis of Gaul and Palmerin of England. Their sports were a mimicry of war, and Francis was always the most valiant, skilful, and bold. He was constantly in danger through his imprudence; two years before, springing on a horse the Maréchal de Gié had given him, he was carried across the fields with such alarming speed that those standing by thought he must be killed; but he kept his seat in spite of the leaps and bounds of the spirited animal. Every day he was exposed to like perils, but escaped harm in a marvellous manner. After having played at "escaigne" (a kind of football), exercised with a bow, or hunted with a net, Francis would divide his companions into two bands, the besiegers and the besieged, and a fierce struggle would follow. These children were skilful at an early age in riding and warlike exercises; they handled swords, pikes, and other implements of war, raised and bore heavy burdens, accustomed themselves to fatigue, and familiarised themselves with military life. Sometimes young Francis would have ambitious dreams, and his comrades, who had not spared him in their games, became his courtiers and flatterers. One day Montmorency, Monchenu, and Brion asked him what positions he would give them when he should become king. Francis, proud of his future prospect, replied, with royal generosity, that they must choose beforehand what office they would prefer. Montmorency said he would like to be Connétable, Monchenu, Admiral, but Brion—more modest in his choice—said he would like to be maître d'hôtel. Twenty-three years afterwards the wishes of all three were realised.

The King rejoiced to find his nephew bigger than children of his own age, and in such splendid health. He was so handsome, it was a pleasure to see him, says the chronicler. Louis showed him as much affection as a father for his son, and greatly respected Louise de Savoie, who had so wisely educated the heir to the Crown. The King was not less pleased with Mademoiselle Marguerite, who was still more accomplished in scholarship than her brother, and more advanced than others of her age. He spent a happy convalescence in the company of these two children, and invited them to Plessis-les-Tours with their mother. They stayed with the King about two months, and he was by this time well enough to hunt, so took with him the Duc de Valois, who loved hunting above all other amusements. Louis, however, could not stand the fatigue every day, so prepared an easy sort of hunting which would not be so dangerous for the "gros garçon," by causing the animals caught by his huntsmen in the forest of Chinon to be let loose in the park. Louise and her children remained with the King until the Queen's return to France, when the heir, his mother, and sister left for Amboise.

The peril of death from which Louis had so recently escaped inspired him with the wish to make the succession sure. He was grateful to his people for the love they had shown towards him during his illness, and as a token of his gratitude was eager to fulfil the wish of the nation, that his daughter Claude should marry the heir to the throne. He therefore signed

LOUIS XII.
(Musée de Cluny.)

an order by which he declared it to be his will
that the betrothal should take place as soon as
possible "for the welfare, surety, and maintenance of the public good of his kingdom, and
notwithstanding the marriage previously agreed
to with Charles Duc de Luxembourg." He
did more than this; he secretly assembled the
chief captains of his guard and made them
swear on the Gospel and the Cross to serve
Madame Claude and the Duc de Valois, and if
he should die without an heir, to prevent the
little Princess being carried out of the kingdom.
Stuart d'Aubigny swore "on the damnation of
his soul and the share he hoped to have in
Paradise" that he and his hundred Scotch
archers would keep this oath even unto death.
His lieutenant, Jean Stuart, captain of the
hundred Swiss, and Guillaume de la Marck
and his lieutenant swore to the same effect.

Louis had to endure painful struggles with
his "Bretonne," who, always obstinate, in wishing her daughter to make an alliance with the
House of Austria, did not cease to urge him to
carry out the treaty of 1501. At first he refused
with jesting remarks, and said to the Queen in

the familiar language he loved to use, that he had resolved "to marry his mice to none but the rats of his barn." Anne replied impatiently: "It would seem, to hear you, that all mothers had conspired together for the harm of their daughters." Louis stood firm and replied, still in figurative language but more seriously, "Do you think there is no difference between your daughter's ruling over little Brittany under the authority of the Kings of France and being the wife of a very powerful King and sharing with him a noble and flourishing kingdom? Which would you prefer, the pack-saddle of an ass or the saddle of a horse?" Far from giving way to these good reasons, Anne persisted with greater ardour; and Louis, without losing his temper, told her the fable of the hind to whom God had given horns, but afterwards took them away because she wished to use them to attack the stag.

Wishing to oppose the express wish of the people to the objections of the Queen, Louis received the deputies of the three Estates in solemn audience. Some historians assert, with probability, that the following scene was prepared by the King and his councillors, but however that may be, the alliance with Francis was certainly popular with the whole nation.

On Thursday the 14th of May 1506 the King of France received the deputies at Plessis-les-Tours, seated on the royal throne, having on his right the Cardinal d'Amboise, the Cardinal de Narbonne, the Chancellor, and many Archbishops and Bishops, and on his left, the Duc de Valois, all the princes of the blood royal, the lords and barons of the kingdom, the President of Parliament, and many councillors. Then a doctor of Paris, Thomas Brico, explained to the King that they had come before him in all humility and reverence to tell him of certain matters greatly concerning the good of his person, the benefit and welfare of his kingdom, and of all Christendom, reminding him that in the month of April of the past year he had been very seriously ill, and that all in his kingdom had been in great fear of losing him, that recognising the great good he had already done in maintaining his people in such peace that they had never been in greater tranquillity, that he had freed his people from a quarter of the taxes, reformed the laws of his kingdom, and set up good judges everywhere, and for other reasons which would be too long to quote, they desired he should henceforth be called "King Louis XII., Father of his people." After this Brico and the deputies fell on their knees, and Brico said: "Sire, we have come here with your good pleasure to make a request for the general good of your kingdom, which is that your very humble subjects beg that it may please you to give Madame, your only daughter, in marriage to Monsieur François here present, who is 'tout français.'" He also said many fine things which moved the King and those present to tears.

After this request the King took the advice of his Council, which was unanimous on the point, and a few days afterwards the Chancellor of France, De Gancy, replied to the deputies of the three Estates that the King, on hearing their petition, had determined as soon as possible to marry his daughter Claude to François d'Angoulême, heir to his crown. Louis remained steadfast in this resolution, though the

Archduke Philip, hearing of the assembly at Plessis, sent remonstrances through his ambassador, reminding Louis of the engagement he had already made.

On Ascension Day, 1506, in the great hall of the Castle of Plessis-les-Tours, the ceremony of betrothal between Claude of France and François d'Angoulême took place. The young Prince was twelve years old, and Claude not quite six.

In the despatch which the ambassador of the Archduke addressed to his master, informing him that the ceremony of betrothal had taken place, he said that the Queen was not at all pleased with what had just happened. In fact, Anne never grew resigned about it, she never spoke of it, but always hoped that some unforeseen event might occur to prevent the marriage. In fact, the only serious quarrel between Louis and Anne was caused by this betrothal; for soon afterwards she went on a visit to Brittany, and prolonged her stay to such an extent that the King was grieved, and later much annoyed, when he heard that she proposed to stay at Rennes for the whole month of September

because "la on devoit faire beaucoup de joûtes."
On the 14th of September the Cardinal
d'Amboise wrote thus to the Queen : " Madame,
the King summoned me to his presence this
afternoon, and I have never seen him so angry,
as you may also hear from Gaspar, to whom he
spoke before me." He ends by urging the
Queen to hasten her return, in order to pacify
the King and to prevent gossip about her
absence. Four days afterwards, the Cardinal,
in reply to assurances Anne had given him
that she would return as soon as the jousts
were over, wrote again : "Although I am
exceedingly glad to hear that you will do all
you can to return to the Court as soon as
possible, I am also, Madame, much grieved
that you do not specify the date of your arrival.
I do not know what to say to the King, who is
greatly concerned about it. Would to God I
was with you to tell you what is said about
your long absence in many places. . . . I will
say no more, except that it grieves me deeply
that you and the King do not speak more
frankly to one another." When the Queen
was at last on her way back, a messenger from

the Cardinal brought a letter, saying: "For God's sake, Madame, do not let these little misunderstandings arise between you; for if they continue you will lose all confidence in, and love for one another, not to speak of the unhappiness which must follow and the mockery of all Christendom." He went on to say that he hoped the Queen, through her good sense, would settle all things amicably, and told her that the King was only eager to welcome her as though nothing had happened. He wrote at the end, "Please burn these letters." Louis, who was goodness itself, had pardoned his "Bretonne" before she had even asked for forgiveness.

Louis cannot be too much praised for resisting the obstinate wish of the Queen-Duchess, for what might not have become of France if the Princess Claude had married Charles of Luxembourg, and added Brittany to the many States already under his sway, when he became Emperor under the title of Charles v.

CHAPTER VI

THE year 1507 found the King entirely preoccupied with preparations for another expedition into Italy—this time to punish the
rebellious Genoese. After a tender farewell
of the Queen, he left Grenoble on Easter
Monday, accompanied, at her request, by Jean
Marot of Caen, who was to write in verse a true
narrative of the journey to Genoa.

During his absence Anne was very anxious
about her little daughter Claude, at this time
little more than seven years old, and her only
child. In April she was attacked by a fever,
which the doctors declared incurable; but in

spite of their sinister predictions her health was restored. The Queen refused to see them any more, and forbade them to approach her child. When, two months later, she left Blois for Grenoble in order to meet the King returning from Genoa, she forbade the Dame de Tournon, the Princess's governess, to let any doctor come near : "My friend," she wrote from Grenoble on the 11th of June, "I have received your letters with good news of my little daughter, for which I am very glad ; let me hear constantly. . . . She must have nothing to do with doctors, and you will, I know, watch over her always as you have done hitherto." Anne preferred to follow the advice given her by the holy Bishop of Grenoble, Laurent Lallemand, uncle of the Chevalier Bayard, and dedicate the little Princess in her prayers to the blessed François de Paule, who had been dead only three weeks. Her prayers were granted, for very soon she heard of the complete recovery of her child. She, however, still wrote constantly to Madame du Bouchage to thank her for her care of the little Princess, and to beg her to send news every day.

A Twice Crowned Queen

Anne, happy and free from anxiety, welcomed Louis at Grenoble in July 1507, and great was her joy at seeing her beloved husband again. She spent several weeks with him either at Grenoble or Lyons, but was at length obliged to return to Blois to prepare for her confinement, after endeavouring to persuade Louis to leave the south and come with her to see their little daughter. Every precaution was taken that her journey from Lyons to Blois should be as easy as possible. Her litter was carried on the shoulders of the King's Swiss soldiers, who were relieved by others at the different resting-places on the route. However, at the end of August, Louis, weary of waiting for a declaration of war, joined the Queen at Blois. The hope of having a son kept him in France and filled him with joy, although he was always wanting to return to Italy.

On the 21st day of January 1508, Anne was delivered of a still-born son. Louise de Savoie has thus recorded this sad birth in her journal: "Anne, Queen of France, had a son on St. Agnes Day, January 21st, at Blois, but he cannot prevent the exaltation of my Cæsar, for he had no life."

In spite of this unfortunate event, Anne could not bring herself to look favourably on the idea of leaving her Duchy to a collateral heir, and doubtless, in order to interest Heaven in her most ardent wish, she founded, enriched, and protected monasteries, especially the Minimes de Nigeon, at Chaillot, near Paris. In her manor of Nigeon she also built a church dedicated to "Nôtre Dame de toutes les Graces." She constantly prayed for a dauphin, and made it a special request on her many pilgrimages; she also invoked Saint René d'Angers and all the saints capable, as was then believed, of giving children to barren women.

The Court, which had deserted the Comtesse d'Angoulême during the time before the Queen's confinement, now returned to her as to the mother of their future King, the young Francis Duc de Valois. François de Montpensier had hastened from Blois to Amboise to inform Louise, waiting impatiently and anxiously there, of the result of the confinement, and never did she nor the Duc de Valois forget the "very humble and loyal service" which he had rendered in bringing them the good tidings so quickly. Louis XII. and the princes of the Court henceforth treated Francis as the heir to the crown.

Louis, during this stay at Blois, very nearly lost all hope for the royal succession in his House, through accidents to Anne and to Francis. On the 6th of August 1508, Francis, who three days before had left his mother at Amboise, in order to take the position his rank assigned him at the Court, and finish his education in the society of lords and ladies, was struck with a stone in the garden at Fontevrault, where he was walking between seven and eight o'clock in the evening, and the wound he received on his forehead made him seriously ill. On the next day the Queen, who was returning from Fontevrault to Montsoreau in her litter, saw the boards of a wooden bridge, over which she was crossing, give way under the feet of her horses, and she remained suspended on the edge of a large opening, where her "attelage" had disappeared, and narrowly escaped from being herself drowned in the Loire.

On the 28th of August the King went to Rouen, whither the Queen followed him on the 3rd of October following. She had been busy seeing after the beautiful monument which she had caused to be erected in the Cathedral of Nantes to the memory of her father and mother.

At the end of February 1509, Louis left Blois for Lyons, with the Queen, princes, and Court. He travelled by easy stages, passing the time in hunting and shooting, the better to hide from the Queen the fact that his army was expecting him beyond the mountains for the expedition against the Venetians, which had been arranged with Maximilian at Cambrai. This league, signed in December 1508, was the cause of keen anxiety to Anne, because her husband was in arms against the holy Father, Julius II. From Lyons the King and Queen journeyed to Grenoble, where Louis left the Queen and Francis. The latter was eager to go on this expedition, but Anne, whose tears and grief could not keep her husband in France, wisely resisted the wishes of the heir, ever too ready to endanger his life.

They returned to Lyons and remained there in order to hear news of Louis as quickly as possible. Anne spent her time chiefly in imploring divine protection for her husband; processions constantly defiled through the streets, where the people crowded round the reliquaries which were followed by men denuded of clothing by way of penance; Anne herself, clothed in mourning, was constantly in tears, and visited the churches attended by her maids of honour, who walked barefoot in the mud. A herald-at-arms brought her letters from the King three days after the victory of Agnadello, and her joy was as great as her anxiety had been—a joy reciprocated by the whole of France. A Te Deum was sung in Paris on the 22nd of May, and the shrine of St. Geneviève was carried in a solemn procession, followed by members of Parliament and the Corporation of the city. Eight days after, the processions recommenced because Louis had sent two Venetian standards to be placed in Saint Denis, "as a token of victory and in perpetual memory." At Lyons the fêtes and rejoicings were animated by the presence of the Queen, who again donned her gay garments, tired her hair, and decked herself with rings, collars, and chains of gold. She headed a procession to the church of St. Jean, which was followed by a great number of nobles on richly caparisoned horses, and by a multitude of the people.

On the 26th of July 1509, Louis left Milan to return to France, urged to do so not only by letters and messengers sent by Anne, but also by the verses of the royal poets who became the interpreters of the Queen's desire to see her husband. Faustus Andrelinus expressed the conjugal grief of Anne in Latin, which Cretin translated into French verse with a naïveté not unpleasing to the Queen. The King, however, was detained ten days at Biagrasso by a tertian fever, which his doctors, Salomon de Bombelles and André Buan, cured by the aid of good diet. He started, still suffering, but eager to see his wife, who, beside herself with grief on hearing of the King's illness, shut herself in her room for eight days and mingled her tears with her prayers so that she might be assured of the safety of her lord. He would not rest anywhere, however, until he reached Saint Denis, because he had made a vow to return thanks to God, in presence of the relics exposed on the altar, for his safe return from Italy and recovery from illness. The Queen met him three leagues from Grenoble, and after making "grande chère," Louis started the next day for Paris. On the way he was met by the Duc de Valois and his tutor; the King embraced Francis, and said he was a "handsome fellow." He was so impatient to fulfil his vow that he would not even have stopped at Blois to see his daughter Claude, who was his treasure and all his "soulas" in this world, had not an attack of gout seized him at Saint-Pierre-le-Moûtier, which obliged him to retire to Blois by the shortest route. The sight of his only child was a great consolation to him. During the whole journey he had refused to devote a single hour to the seductions of the chase or shooting, sports which he much enjoyed; nevertheless his vow was not accomplished until the following year.

In December 1509, Marguerite, the sister of Francis, was married to Charles d'Alençon. The Princess was now seventeen, and celebrated for her wit, beauty, and intelligence. The King and Queen honoured the marriage with as much pomp and ceremony as if it had been that of their own child, and everyone noticed what favour Louis XII. showed them. Marguerite herself, who had submitted to the will of her mother in taking a husband, directed her thoughts towards Heaven for consolation, and gave her heart to God since her husband had it not. The joy of Francis, who loved the Duc d'Alençon as a companion of his childhood, was not less keen than that of Louis. The bride was conducted by the King to the chapel of the Castle of Blois, where Mass was sung by the Archbishop of Sens, and afterwards he led her into the banqueting hall, where the Queen sat in the centre of the table, surrounded by princesses and ambassadors who—admitted to the Queen's table— were served on gold plate but ate in common.

A Twice Crowned Queen

Anne, the bride, and the old Duchesse de Bourbon had each her "plat à part." The Queen then gave the heralds a large silver-gilt vase, and they cried "Largesse, largesse," according to the custom of chivalry. After the banquet, dances began until the time for the tournament, in which Monseigneur the Duc de Valois fought with Gaston de Foix, Duc de Nemours, and four other knights. It was the first time Francis had shown his skill at Court; but, during the absence of the King, Anne had often watched the Prince at his warlike exercises, had admired his spirit, and talked to him in "fine and virtuous words." On this day, Francis appeared in the lists clad in cloth of gold; and the King, wearing the same, stood as "parrain" in his first joust, presented him with his lance, and did not leave him until he had finished his strokes. The next day and the day after combats on foot and on horseback continued, and the ladies were ordered to give the prize to the most worthy. The Duc de Valois, in spite of his youth, proved the most valiant of all the company.

A Twice Crowned Queen

Anne, whose religion was a blind faith entirely subject to the will of her confessor, Yves de Maheuc, looked with bitter grief on the quarrels of her husband with the Pope. She hated the schism between the Church in France and Rome, and redoubled her efforts to make peace between the King and the Pope. She grieved at the persecutions which the Chief of Christendom had to suffer, and Louis replied to her pious complaints by one of those quick and witty remarks in which deep sense is hidden under a gay and satirical form. "The holy Father aims at royal honours," he said gravely; "St. Peter had not the leisure to look after the affairs of Claudius or Nero, which in truth do not belong to him at all." Louis for a long time firmly resisted the religious scruples of the Queen, but gradually gave way, as will be seen, through affection for his dear "Bretonne."

On the 25th of October 1510, the Queen gave birth to her second daughter, Renée, and the hopes of the King and the whole nation were again disappointed. Informed at La Herronière of the approach of the confinement, and seeing that all he had undertaken in Italy that season was accomplished, Louis hastened to Lyons, starting before it was day, and made such good progress by land and water that he arrived at Blois in four or five days, and those who could not travel so fast remained behind. On his arrival he found the Queen near her delivery, and "no people knew how to welcome each other better than they did," they made "si bonne chère" when they were together. The King was in the room during the birth, the chronicler tells us, and adds that this was very virtuous of him, "because there is no greater pain than to see anyone one loves suffer."

This Princess Renée afterwards married Ercole d'Este Duke of Ferrara. She was plain and slightly deformed, but learned and a great talker, fond of astrology and metaphysics, and favoured the cause of the Reformation.

The child was called Renée in gratitude to St. René, patron saint of Angers, for the King and Queen had made several pilgrimages to obtain offspring, and had visited the relics of this holy

Bishop. The Marshal de Trivulce, who was
honoured by being chosen to "lever l'enfant,"
came post-haste from Lombardy and had to
return immediately after the baptism. The
Dowager Duchesse de Bourbon and Madame
du Bouchage were godmothers, and held
Madame Renée at the font with Trivulce. It is
said that Anne was not properly treated during
this confinement, and that she was always ailing
afterwards. During the month of March 1511
the Queen had a serious illness, which placed
her life in danger. De Burgo, Margaret of
Austria's ambassador at the Court of France,
wrote thus to his mistress's secretary : "The
Queen, as I lately informed Madame, was
nearly well again, but last night she was
suddenly attacked with fever and other
symptoms so violently that her life was in
danger." Later on, he wrote that the patient
had had such a bad night, she had lost all
power of speech, but after having received the
last Sacraments she gradually became better.
Anne indeed recovered, and on the 4th of April
following, De Burgo wrote the news of her
convalescence.

Anne would not allow the Church in Brittany to take any part in the Council of Pisa, but openly rose against the schismatical assembly and adhered to the Council of the Lateran, convened by Pope Julius II., to counteract the dangerous effects of the former, at which he himself was cited to appear in person. The King, however, remained firm; and much as he loved his wife, did not yield though her incessant solicitations were accompanied by caresses and tears. During the quarrel between the Pope and her husband Anne redoubled her pious practices, as though to expiate the King's heresy; she lavished alms on the religious orders, especially on the "Filles Pénitentes de Paris" and the "Minimes" of Nigeon, to induce them to remember Louis in their prayers; she expelled the Jews, and gave pensions from her treasury to those who consented to receive baptism; she founded a stately convent of "Cordeliers" at Lyons and many other monasteries; she sent presents to the churches; ordered reliquaries of gold and precious stones; embroidered with her own hand, assisted by her ladies, numbers of ecclesiastical garments; she commanded her artists to paint missals and books of Hours, and to ornament the margins with flowers instead of the monsters and grotesques which figured in the manuscripts of the day; she was constantly surrounded by priests and monks that she might be enlightened by their wisdom and confide in them her griefs, and she did not leave her oratory except to kiss relics at various places of pilgrimage, and carry her anxiety for Louis' salvation from chapel to chapel. After such a visit she would return to the King more pressing and desolate than ever, and beg him to give up the hated Council and submit to the Pope. One day the King's patience was sorely tried by the anathemas which Anne uttered against the Council of Pisa : "Eh quoi! Madame," he said to her in anger, "cuidez vous être plus docte et mieux apprise que tant de célèbres Universités qui ont ce Concile approuvé? Vos confesseurs ne vous ont-ils point dit que les femmes n'avaient point de voix dans les choses de l'Eglise?"

On the 23rd of January 1512, Jean Leveau wrote to Margaret of Austria : "The day before yesterday, which was the 21st of this month, at three o'clock in the afternoon, the Queen was delivered of a still-born son, much to the King's grief, though others take it calmly since God wills it thus." This last unhappy confinement was followed by serious consequences, and in the following March Anne again had fever, and did not leave her bed until May. De Burgo gave his mistress an account of an audience he had with Anne on the 19th of May : " Madame, although the Queen is not yet quite well and speaks to no stranger, she was pleased to wish to see me, to hear what the Emperor had written to me about some days ago, and that I might take leave of her; I found her in bed, but looking well and much improved in health."

Soon afterwards the Queen proposed a visit to Brittany, not only to show herself to her dear Bretons and encourage them vigorously to repulse the maritime attacks of the English, but to pay her vows at the renowned places of pilgrimage, especially at the church of Nôtre Dame de Folgoët and the chapel of Sainte Anne d'Auray. During the serious illness which placed her husband's life in danger in 1505, she had dedicated him to the Virgin of Folgoët, and she herself never failed to invoke her patron St. Anne whenever, in trying circumstances of her life, she needed divine intervention. The King probably succeeded in dissuading her from this journey because of the still delicate nature of her health.

Anne, whose religious scruples and pious terrors had caused much trouble and hesitation in the management of public and political affairs, at last induced the King to relax his, till now inflexible, resolution, and to consent to allow her intervention with the Pope to take its course. The Cardinal who was charged with this delicate mission had no sooner mentioned Louis' name than Julius turned his back on the intermediary of the Queen of France. In a decree of the 10th of December 1512, the Pope, in his turn, had summoned the King to appear at the Lateran Council with all those who had adhered to the schismatical Council of Pisa. This order for a penitential appearance caused Anne fresh alarm; she begged the Cardinal de Luxembourg, who was much esteemed at the Court of Rome, to address a supplication to the Lateran Council for the reconciliation of the King of France with the Pope, abjuring his conduct with regard to the Council of Pisa, and begging the holy Father to pardon him ; but if pardon should be refused to the King, who was making "amende honorable," they dared to hope that His Holiness would deign to look with favour on the Dauphin Francis, successor to the throne, and on the Queen who solicited this pardon with tears in her eyes. Julius had no time to receive the submission of his redoubtable enemy. Attacked by a slow fever which sapped his strength, he began, as his last moments drew nigh, to feel remorse : "Would to God!" he cried, "that I had not been Pope, or that I had employed the arms I turned against Christendom against the infidel!" he died on the night of the 21st of February 1513, at the age of seventy.

Louis was displeased when Leo x. succeeded, because he had secretly contributed to the support of Maximilian Sforza, son of Lodovico and Beatrice d'Este, in his Duchy of Milan, and continued to pay the Swiss to guard Piedmont in case of an offensive return of the French army. The King forbade money to be sent to the Court of Rome, and thus considerably reduced the revenue of the Holy See. The new Pope did not wish, at least openly, to declare himself against the most Christian King, whom he had not yet released from excommunication, but proposed an amicable agreement, and secretly employed in his interest the pious intervention of Anne, who exercised an active influence not only over the King, but also over his Ministers. For more than four years Anne pursued this end with indefatigable zeal and perseverance, and it was she who accomplished the reconciliation of Louis with the Pope and the Church.

About this time the Queen realised one of her dearest hopes when she persuaded the King to sign a treaty of marriage for her second daughter, Renée, with the Prince of Castile, Archduke of Austria. She was never able, however, to gain his consent to the alliance of this Prince with his eldest daughter Claude. The King promised as dowry the Duchy of Milan, the County of Asti, and the lordship of Genoa if Renée should espouse one of the two Princes of Castile, Charles or Ferdinand. The Queen's ambition in this respect was directed and sustained by the hatred she felt for Louise de Savoie, and before Louis had even consented to the alliance of his youngest daughter, Anne sent to her niece, Germaine de Foix Queen of Aragon, the Sieur de Brèves, giving him full power to treat not only for the marriage of the Princess Renée with the Archduke Ferdinand, but also for an amicable understanding between the King of France and the King of Spain. Anne, alas! never had the happiness of seeing this darling project of her heart realised. She had not been in good health since her last confinement, and for many years past, indeed, she had been always more or less ailing, which is not surprising when one recollects at what a tender age she had to battle against the difficulties of life and suffer many hardships. Though both her marriages were happy in themselves, they brought her sad and grievous sorrow in the death of so many of her children; her unfortunate confinements, doubtless greatly mismanaged in those rough days, must have tended to weaken her constitution, and her life, in spite of the splendours of her double reign, was one of continual struggle, which she sustained with the impatience of opposition usual in one accustomed from childhood to being obeyed.

In 1513, Anne was still young, not yet thirty-eight, and there was hope of the King's joy being complete in having a son of his own to succeed him, but, alas! the chronicler tells us that "the said Queen was often sick with an illness called stone." Towards the end of the year this malady grew suddenly worse. She had summoned to Blois the *Jeune Aventureux*, Robert de la Marck Seigneur de Fleuranges, for some affair connected with the King of Castile and the House of Austria. The Seigneur de Fleuranges having duly arrived at the Queen's orders, she fell ill while talking with him. This violent attack was complicated by an intermittent fever, which the doctors, however, did not consider dangerous. The Queen herself did not think seriously of her condition, for soon afterwards she again sent for Robert de la Marck and begged him not to leave Blois until she was well again. She was still in treaty for the marriage of her daughter Renée with one of the princes of Castile. But she rapidly grew worse, and began to prepare for a holy death by pardoning her enemies; in proof of which she bequeathed the administration of her goods, her fortune, and the care of her daughters to Louise de Savoie, Comtesse d'Angoulême, whom she had more than once offended, and had always treated with unconcealed dislike.

On Monday the 9th of January 1514, Anne of Brittany, after ten days of acute suffering, which the doctors could not relieve, gave up her soul to God, and passed away from the cares and anxieties of this earthly life. "Her death was a great loss to many good people," says the Sieur de Fleuranges, who adds this sad revelation, "but there was one who was very glad, and that was Monseigneur d'Angoulême, because she had always been opposed to his plans and wishes, and there was never a time when these two Houses were not at feud."

The chroniclers of the time maintain that Anne fell a victim to the ignorance and mismanagement of her doctors; and those in attendance on the Queen said they were greatly to be blamed, and ought to be dismissed from the Court.

Anne of Brittany died in a room of the old Castle of Blois which she had always occupied since her marriage with Charles VIII., and which is still one of the objects of interest in that grand building. Here her body remained from Monday until the following Friday night, the surgeons and apothecaries having meanwhile embalmed it, and, according to the last wish of the Queen, they extracted her heart, which was enclosed in a golden box. She knew that her body would be taken to Saint Denis, so she begged that the best part of her remains should be buried at Nantes, in the tomb of her father and mother, and among the Bretons she had loved so well.

The King's grief was great and inconsolable. He was "so afflicted that for eight days he did nothing but weep, wishing continually that it might be God's pleasure to take him also." He begged that the grave might be made large enough for two, for, he said, "devant que l'an soit passé, je serai avec elle."

For five days mendicant friars said the office of the dead round the body, and on Friday night it was borne into a State room, situated in the new part of the Castle. This room was richly hung with silk tapestry representing the destruction of Jerusalem ; the lower part of the walls was now hung with black velvet decorated with the escutcheon and device of the Queen, a golden girdle. The Queen's body, dressed in royal garments, was placed on a State bed covered with cloth of gold bordered with ermine. The crown was placed on her head, and her sceptre and wand of justice on cushions of cloth of gold at her side.

The dead Queen remained thus with her face uncovered from Saturday till Monday evening, surrounded by monks, who never ceased to say Masses and other prayers for the dead. She was visited by princes and princesses of her family, by her ladies and maids of honour, and by all the officials and members of her household clad in mourning garments. Everyone, on seeing the face which death had in no wise changed, cried and sobbed and uttered piteous lamentation. It was a sad sight when on Monday evening the Queen's body, which had being lying thus in State for three days, had to be disturbed and placed in a wooden coffin lined with lead, covered outside with copper on which was engraved a long epitaph. Tears and lamentations began afresh when a veil was thrown over the Queen's face; some kissed the coffin, others the shroud, and the noble face was uncovered several times. The sobs and groans lasted so long that some were obliged to go away, saying, "There lies our Queen and mistress, let us pray to God for her."

Every day four high Masses were chanted by the prelates and choir of the royal chapel, in addition to those said by the monks, the funeral ceremonies lasting fifteen days.

The performance of all these sad functions must have told heavily on the bereaved King and on all who took part in them, but the saddest day of all must have been when, on Friday the 3rd of February, about two o'clock in the afternoon, the body of the Queen was borne by officers of her household from the hall of mourning to the church of St. Sauveur, outside the Castle, preceded and followed by a numerous procession of clergy and monks, the poor of the town, members of her household, officials of the Duchy of Brittany, and the Grand Master of the King's house. The royal princes and princesses also followed, François d'Angoulême, heir to the throne, clothed in a long mourning garment which had a train more than three yards long.

Masses were said the following morning, and Maître Guillaume Parvi, the Queen's confessor, pronounced the first part of the funeral oration which was to be continued at Paris and finished at Saint Denis. About two o'clock the coffin was placed on a four-wheeled carriage, covered with a black velvet pall crossed with white satin and falling down to the ground; it was drawn by six handsome horses caparisoned with black velvet and white satin so that only their eyes could be seen; two knights on horseback led the procession in front of the bier, six of the King's archers kept the way on either side to prevent the crowd from coming too near, and the Swiss guards lined the way. The funeral cortège stopped at all the chief towns on the route where services were held. The people went in crowds before the procession and knelt by the wayside praying God for the Queen-Duchess, remembering that she had never come among them without leaving substantial tokens of her love behind her, and in order to prolong her bounty still her almoners distributed money to the poor of the towns and villages through which the late Queen's body passed. On Monday the 13th the body remained at the abbey of Nôtre - Dame - des - Champs outside the gates of Paris, and on Tuesday at mid-day the procession again set out towards the cathedral of Nôtre Dame ; the streets of Paris were hung with black, tan, or blue, and the inhabitants had set lighted torches before the doors of their houses ; each square and street leading on to the Rue Saint Denis was guarded to prevent overcrowding ; the various public bodies of the city, the provost's archers, town-criers, watchmen, monks, and clergy joined the procession. The royal princes and princesses had followed from Blois mounted on little black mules caparisoned with velvet, the ladies and maids of honour on horses led two by two by a groom on foot.

The Queen's coffin was borne into the cathedral by officers of her household, who were weeping or uttering deep groans; the four corners of the pall were carried by the four presidents of Parliament. The porch, as well as the interior of the vast edifice, was hung with black cloth, on which were embroidered the arms of the Queen; in the midst of the choir a "chapelle ardente," lighted by twelve hundred candles, was erected, and on this the body was placed; the high altar and all the side altars were draped in black velvet and white silk, and the candles burning on these altars numbered three thousand eight hundred.

On Wednesday the 15th of February, when all had taken their places, a solemn Mass was said by the Cardinal de Mans, and the second part of the funeral oration was delivered. After this service all went to dine, but with sorrowful hearts, grieving at their irreparable loss. In the afternoon the twenty-four criers dispersed through the town, saying: " Honourable and devout persons, pray for the soul of the most noble, most powerful, very excellent, generous, and benevolent Princess Anne, in her lifetime by the grace of God, Queen of France, Duchess of Brittany, who died at the Castle of Blois on the 9th day of February, and now lies in the church of Nôtre Dame. Say your paternosters that God may have mercy on her soul."

[January

On the same day the procession wended its way to Saint Denis, the princes and princesses going on foot as far as the church of St. Lazare outside the city walls, where they mounted their mules. On the arrival at the royal abbey the body was placed on the catafalque prepared for it in the choir of the church. The next day, Thursday, a solemn Mass was held, and Guillaume de Parvi finished the funeral discourse. He began with the words, "Cecidit corona capitis nostri," and spoke of the fabulous genealogy which carried the Queen back to Madame Inoge, wife of Brutus and daughter of Pindarus the Trojan. He told the following legendary story of the famous ermine, found at Troisic, now Le Croisic, in Brittany. During a hunting expedition an ermine was pursued by the dogs of King Brutus, and taking refuge in the lap of Inoge, she saved it from death, fed it for a long time, and adopted an ermine as her badge.

When the Cardinal de Mans rose to give the benediction, the magnificent jewelled cope, embroidered by Anne and her ladies, was placed on his shoulders. It had been presented by her to the church of the great patron of France where her body was finally to rest.

After the absolution, the saddest of all the sad ceremonies took place when the coffin was lowered into a vault before the high altar which Louis had had prepared for himself and his wife since his second marriage. This vault was eight feet long and eight feet wide, and at one end, in a niche, was a marble and gold statue of Our Lady, with the arms of France on the right and those of Brittany on the left. The coffin rested on bars of iron two feet from the ground.

When the Cardinal had thrown a little earth on the tomb, the Champagne King-at-Arms advanced, called three times for silence, and

said : " Bretagne King-at-Arms, do your duty."
Then the King-at-Arms of the Bretons cried
out : " The most Christian Queen-Duchess our
Sovereign Lady and Mistress is dead. The
Queen is dead. The Queen is dead." Then at
a summons from the King-at-Arms, the
Gentleman-Usher came forward, bearing the
rod of justice, the Grand Master of Brittany the
sceptre, and the Master of the Horse the
crown. After having respectfully kissed the
insignia, they delivered them into the hands of
" Bretagne," who, kissing them in his turn,
placed them on the coffin.

The people were then allowed to approach,
and reverently with tears and sighs they
did so, each testifying aloud to his grief and
regret before kneeling to say a short prayer.
Throughout the whole of the next day crowds
from all parts were constantly pouring along
the road from Paris to Saint Denis in order to
visit the royal tomb.

The only act of the sad obsequies still to be
gone through was the funeral feast, which took
place on the same day, Saturday, the 18th of
February. It was of the most magnificent

description, and carried out under the direction of Monsieur de Menou, first maître d'hôtel of the late Queen. The President of Parliament, a great number of noted persons, and all the officials of the Queen's household were present. Jean de Bretagne Baron d'Avaugour, Anne's natural brother, presided in his office of Grand Master of Brittany. After the repast he rose and, addressing those present, said, "Messeigneurs, the most Christian Queen and Duchess, our Sovereign Lady and Mistress, loved you much and was ever mindful of your welfare. You served her loyally. It has pleased God to take her away from us. If I can do you any favour generally or individually, I will undertake it willingly. You may betake you to the service of the King or to that of Mesdames, his daughters. That you may know the household exists no longer, I break this rod,"

Then the Brittany King-at-Arms said with a loud voice: "The most Christian Queen and Duchess, our Sovereign Lady and Mistress, is dead, let each provide for himself."

For many years this funeral, with its numerous ceremonies, served as a guide to the

A Twice Crowned Queen

Court on similar occasions, and Louis ordered Pierre Choque, the Brittany King-at-Arms, and a most devoted servant of the Queen, to give a faithful and detailed account of the obsequies, authorising him to have a certain number of copies transcribed to perpetuate the memory of the sad event. Jean de Paris painted eleven miniatures, representing the principal scenes of the funeral, which were copied into each account. The King ordered his mourning to be in black, as Anne had done after the death of her first husband, and all who approached him, princes, ambassadors, courtiers, and servants, were to be clad in mourning garments. For several weeks games, dances, and plays were strictly prohibited. All joy and happiness seemed to have gone out of Louis' life, but he rallied to make a fresh effort to push his favourite plan—the marriage of Claude and Francis. It took place the same year, and both bride and bridegroom were in black, he— unwilling, she — submissive. His only wedding gifts to her were a four-post bed and a counterpane. There were no trumpets or feasting, "pas un ombre de drap d'or ou de soie." Louise de Savoie was not present, and after dinner the bridegroom went hunting in the Park as usual—a wedding day which seems an epitome of the poor little bride's existence. She was sweet-looking but uninteresting, and little calculated to retain the affections of a husband so gallant, inconstant, and fond of pleasure. Anne had feared this; but Louis, with that goodness so uniformly visible in his character, replied to her remonstrances, "Vous vous trompez, elle n'est pas belle, mais sa vertu touchera le Comte, et il ne pourra s'empêcher de lui rendre justice." Francis, however, hardly justified this favourable opinion of him.

Those about the Court soon forgot the respect due to the memory of Anne of Brittany. One day, at the King's Council, someone dared to speak slightingly of the late Queen. Guy de Laval, who was present, and to whom Anne had married the Princesse de Tarente, daughter of Frederick III., the deposed King of Naples, rose indignantly and said: "I do not know why you thus speak. Remember that since the foundation of your kingdom, you never had a Queen who was so great a lady, nor one who enriched you more. Show me an acre of land your other queens have brought you. Her memory ought to be venerated above that of all other; through her you Bretons have lost the enemies who kept you in the heart of the Duchy whenever it pleased the Dukes her predecessors who kept the key of your gates." These dignified words made both French and Breton courtiers more circumspect in their attitude towards the late Queen. Anne herself had always had a presentiment that her memory would not last long among the French. She had never been in true sympathy with them, and they had resented her strong preference for Brittany. Knowing this, she had given orders that her heart should be buried in the tomb of Francis II. at Nantes. It was therefore placed in a golden heart surmounted by a crown and encircled with her device, the nun's girdle. The inscriptions inside and out were in letters of white enamel. Inside, the following lines were written :—

" O cuer chaste et pudique, ô juste et begnin cuer,
Cuer magnanyme et franc, de tous vices vainqueur,
O cuer digne entre tous de couronne celeste,
Or est ton cler esprit hors de peine at moleste."

A Twice Crowned Queen

Outside the heart were two quatrains :
On one side

"En ce petit vaisseau
De fin or pur et munde
Repose ung plus grand cueur
Que oncques Dame eut au monde
Anne fut le nom d'elle
En France deux fois Reine
Duchesse des Bretons
Royale et Souveraine."

M . V̊ . XIII.

And on the other :

" Ce cuer fut si tres hault
Que de la terre aux cieux
Sa vertu liberalle
Accroissoit mieulx et mieulx
Mais Dieu en a reprins
Sa portion meilleure
Et ceste part terrestre
En grand deuil nous demeure."
IX. Janvier.

Round the crown were inscribed the words :

" Cueur de vertus orné dignement couronné."

Early in the month of March this heart was
taken to Nantes by several nobles of Brittany,
and on the 13th it was placed with much
ceremony in the Church of the Carthusians at
Nantes, on the tomb of Arthur III. of Brittany,
the Duke who defeated the English at
184

A Twice Crowned Queen

Formigny. On the following Sunday, the 19th, the Queen's heart was transferred to the Church of the Carmelites, where, after a solemn service, surpassing in magnificence those held at Blois, Paris, and Saint Denis, it was placed in a leaden chest within the splendid tomb of Francis II. and Marguerite de Foix. On the 16th of October 1727 this tomb was opened by order of Louis XV. Three leaden coffins with ermines painted on them were found inside. They contained the bodies of Francis and his two wives, and between the coffins of the Duke and Anne's mother was the leaden box enclosing the golden heart.

On the 17th of February 1792 the tomb of Francis II. was again opened by the Revolutionists, its contents dishonoured, and the sculpture mutilated and partially destroyed. In 1819, however, through the energy and care of the Comte de Brosses, Prefect of the Department and Mayor of Nantes, the separate pieces of the tomb, which had been preserved as though by a miracle, were put together and set up in the Cathedral of Nantes to the admiration of all who visit this fine piece of Renaissance work. The leaden box containing the golden heart was broken up, and the golden heart was placed in the Cabinet des Médailles in the National Library ; but at the request of the Municipal Council in 1817 this precious relic was returned to the town of Nantes.

The death of the Queen, together with Francis' marriage, gave a new face to affairs. Louise de Savoie began to display her brilliant but dangerous character, kept under strong restraint during Anne's life, and Louis, grown wise by experience, tender of his people and frugal of the revenues, viewed with a melancholy foresight the luxury and extravagance which the heir's character predicted. In anticipation of the evils which such qualities would probably entail on his kingdom, he used frequently to exclaim, " Ce gros gars-là gâtera tout ! " It is even to be suspected that this formed one of the great motives of his third marriage, though the desire of a close union and alliance with England formed a more ostensible pretext.

Henry VIII. had a sister of uncommon beauty.

A Twice Crowned Queen

The Duc de Longueville, who had been taken prisoner at the battle of Guinegate, being sent over to negotiate a treaty of peace, first opened overtures for this match, which were immediately accepted. The Princess Mary was conducted to France, received at Boulogne by a splendid train, at the head of which was the Comte d'Angoulême, and married at Abbeville to the King. She was in early youth, gay and fond of pleasure; her heart had already engaged itself to a young English lord whom Henry VII. had created Duke of Suffolk, and to whom he had even intended to give his daughter's hand. Under these circumstances it cannot be supposed that Louis, a valetudinarian, sinking into years, worn by the fatigues of war, tormented by the gout, and occupied continually with the recollection of his late Queen, could be a very acceptable husband.

"Francis, amorous and gallant to excess, was captivated by her charms, and it is pretended that he might and would have pushed his good fortune to the utmost length if political considerations and his mother's reprehensions had not, though with difficulty,

187

imposed a restraint on his desires. Most contemporary authors relate very circumstantially an anecdote which, if true, puts it beyond doubt that Francis had gained a most complete and tender interest in the young Queen's affections. Pressed by the importunities of her lover, and yielding to his entreaties, she at length granted him a rendezvous in the Palais des Tournelles, and there can be little question that such an interview would have been decisive. The Count habited himself in the most gallant manner, and was hastening to the Queen's apartments, when he was met by Grignaux, an ancient gentleman who had been in the service of Anne of Brittany. Struck with the more than common magnificence of his dress, knowing his predominant weakness, mistrustful of his intentions, Grignaux rudely stopped him, and addressing him, demanded whither he was going so hastily. 'Donnez-vous en bien garde, Monseigneur,' said he frowning, 'pasques Dieu! vous vous jouez à vous donner un maître; il ne faut qu'un accident pour que vous restiez Comte d'Angoulême toute votre vie.' This bold and peremptory remonstrance was not lost on the person to whom it was directed. Francis paused on the very threshold of his mistress's chamber; love and empire disputed for an instant in his bosom. The latter triumphed, and submitting to Grignaux's counsel, he had either the magnanimity or the weakness to suffer himself to be led away from the temptation and conducted out of the palace." *

The tomb Louis had prepared for Anne was very soon opened, for a few months after this ill-assorted marriage Louis himself died, on the 1st of January 1515. His body was placed beside that of Anne; and the new King, Francis I., ordered the sculptor, Jean Just, to raise a tomb worthy in all respects of the royal majesty of his predecessor.

Louis XII. was thirty-six when he succeeded to the throne of France. His judgment, naturally clear and discerning, was ripened by experience; his heart, full of every gentle and beneficent sentiment, was rendered supremely capable of feeling the calamities of others by those which he had undergone himself. He was the most virtuous Prince that France, perhaps even Europe, ever saw. In the whole palace it was proclaimed at his death, "Le bon

* Wraxall, *Memoirs of the Kings of France.*

A Twice Crowned Queen

Roi Louis XII., Père du Peuple, est mort!" The tears of sorrow and commiseration which he used to shed when the necessities of war obliged him to levy an additional subsidy, however small, on his people, proved how justly he merited the appellation of Father of his people. His clemency, benevolence, and unbounded philanthropy were not inferior to Henry IV.'s, but these benign qualities were not obscured and diminished in him by that unhappy and pernicious passion for women which accompanied the founder of the House of Bourbon to the grave. He was the pattern of conjugal fidelity, and his Court, decent and restrained, neither knew the elegant politeness nor the luxurious gallantry which Francis I. introduced on his accession to the throne. His valour and military capacity had been distinguished in many campaigns. His temper, open and candid, made him easy of access, and he was cheerful and gracious to the highest degree. "The voice of a whole people, their simple and unembellished lamentations, were his best panegyric."*

* Wraxall.

A Twice Crowned Queen

Mézeray says of him : "Quand il allait par les champs les bonnes gens accouraient de plusieurs journées pour le voir, lui jonchant les chemins de fleurs et de feuillages, et comme si c'eût été un Dieu visible essayaient de faire toucher leurs mouchoirs à sa monture pour les garder comme de précieuses reliques."

CHAPTER VII

ALTHOUGH the record of Anne's life has now
been concluded with her untimely death, a few
particulars as to her character, tastes, and
personal appearance may be of interest.

In a portrait in oils which has come down
to us, her face has a refinement and purity of
contour which suggests youthfulness and grace ;
it was probably painted about the time of her
first marriage with Charles VIII., because it bears
a strong resemblance to the head on the gold
medal struck at Lyons on the occasion of the
State entry of the King and Queen in 1493.
As she grew older, the strong Breton type
became more marked, as may be seen in the
miniature of her Book of Hours ; her high

forehead gave majesty to her glance ; her complexion was brilliant, and her large bright eyes were always kept in subjection by the severity of her manners. She was of medium height, and bore herself with much dignity ; her walk, in spite of the slight limp, was quick and imperious. St. Gelais de Monlieu says : " To see her bearing and dignity one would think that the whole world belonged to her, so much so that at first sight people fear to address her ; but, in truth, if one has a little matter and finds opportunity to mention it, no one could be kinder, more approachable and sympathetic ; those who visit her leave her presence rejoicing and satisfied."

Through the various epochs of her career it will have been seen how strong a character she possessed ; her firmness, however, bordered on obstinacy, and she little brooked any contradiction. She was courteous and had much good sense, but her very virtues tended towards prudishness. In a licentious age no whisper of scandal was ever breathed against her. Pious almost to bigotry, she was ever ready to help those in distress, and gave much of her wealth to the poor, for the endowment of schools, convents, and hospitals, and the building, repairing, or enriching of churches and abbeys; in fact the Queen-Duchess was indefatigable in her almsgiving and in her care for others, as the following instances will show.

In August 1498, when she was about to leave Paris after the death of Charles VIII., she was anxious to acknowledge the faithful service Jacques de Tournon had rendered in the management of her establishment there, so ordered £1600 (a considerable sum in those days) to be presented to him.

She gave another esteemed servant, Lope de Dicastillo, 300 Tours pounds to compensate him for the loss of his baggage at the battle of Fornova.

Wishing one of her pages, Guillaume de Saint-Forjeul, whose parents were not wealthy, to take part in a tournament held by the young gentlemen of her Court in July 1498, she gave him £35 to enable him to enter the lists properly equipped.

She never forgot services rendered by Bretons to herself or her father, and by chance

ANNE OF BRITTANY WITH HER PATRON SAINTS,
St. ANNE, St. URSULA, AND St. MARGARET.

(From her Book of Hours (Louvre).

hearing that one of her maîtres-d'hôtel had borrowed £800 from a merchant of Tours to enable him to defend the cause of Duke Francis II. in 1490, she ordered this sum to be paid out of her treasury.

In the interesting chapter which Brantôme has given to Anne of Brittany, he mentions her as being the first Queen to gather round her person a number of young girls of noble family. These girls were watched over with the strictest care; no man was allowed to approach them except in the presence of the Queen, and gouvernantes were appointed to see that rules were obeyed. The luckless Anne Boleyn was for a while at the French Court,* but she resented the strictness of life which the Queen exacted, and in a fit of temper left the Castle and joined the Court of Marguerite d'Angoulême.† Anne of Brittany was always most anxious that her Court should be free from the licence so general at the time,

---

* Edith Sichel, *Women and Men of the French Renaissance.*

† This, however, is doubtful; for from other sources we find that, in 1514, Anne Boleyn accompanied Mary Tudor to France as maid-in-waiting, and after Louis XII.'s death remained in the service of Queen Claude.

but she, no doubt, exceeded the limits of caution by over-severity.

Mrs. Ady, in her interesting life of Isabella d'Este, gives a curious letter written in Anne's own hand to the Marchioness of Mantua, concerning her wish to bring up Isabella's little daughter Leonora at the French Court as one of her maids of honour. Francesco Gonzaga had been spending Christmas 1502 at Loches with the King and Queen of France, and Anne of Brittany renewed an offer she had before made to educate his daughter at her Court and marry her to a prince of the blood-royal. The plan, although it must at one time have been seriously considered, was never carried out. The letter, still preserved in the Gonzaga archives, runs as follows :—

" A MA COUSINE LA MARQUISE DE MANTOVE, —Ma cousine, mon cousin votre mari m'a dit que lui et vous me veuliez bailler votre fille pour estre avec mey et vous la m'envoyerez, mais que eussiez sceu mon vouloir. Ma cousine, envoiez la moi quant vais voudrez, car je la traieteray tout ainsi que si elle estoit myenne, et pouvez estre seure, ma cousine, que tout ce que je pourriez faire pour vous, toujours my employereay de bon cœur. Priant Dieu, ma cousine, qu'il vous ait en sa garde.—Votre bonne cousine,   ANNE.

"ESCRIPT À LOCHES, *le 15 jour Decembre.*"

Her ruling passion was match-making, and she was indefatigable in her efforts to get her maids of honour suitably married. So great was her ardour, that the Pope presented her with an "autel portatif" with permission to bless marriages at any moment. During the Italian wars she was in difficulties as to how she should give the usual dowry of £3000 (Tours) to three of her maids of honour, and in order to do so, generously placed some valuable diamond ornaments in the hands of her bankers at Lyons, which she was unable to redeem until two years later.

In 1500, Ladislaus King of Poland, Bohemia, and Hungary sent ambassadors to Louis XII., among other things to ask for a wife from among the King's relations. Anne immediately suggested two beautiful girls of the House of Foix—either Germaine, Louis' niece, or Anne de Candale. After some hesitation Anne was chosen, and the marriage carried out as soon

197

as possible by proxy. After shedding many
tears the young girl bade farewell to her companions and left France to marry the King
of a distant country. Her grief was great
because she was in love with the Comte de
Dunois, grandson of the famous Bastard of
Orleans; she did all she could to delay her
departure, but the inevitable moment came only
too quickly, though some months had elapsed
since the marriage by proxy. She was accompanied to Buda-Pesth by a brilliant suite of
ladies and gentleman and the Queen's King-
at-Arms, Pierre Choque, who was to give a
detailed account of all that took place on the
journey, and of the establishment of the young
Queen in a country still very little known. The
King and Queen loved Anne as though she
were their own daughter. Alas! this brilliant
union was not of long duration; Anne could
never forget the Court of France nor the happy
marriage of which she had dreamed; she died
within a year from her arrival in Hungary
while giving birth to a son.

In 1505, Germaine de Foix was given in
marriage to Ferdinand of Spain, whose first

wife, Isabella, had died the year before. In a letter sent with the young bride to her new home, Louis speaks of her as "their very dear and much loved daughter."

Another alliance effected by Anne was that of Charlotte d'Aragon Princesse de Tarente, who had refused the hand of Cæsar Borgia. She was a charming girl, large-hearted and witty, beloved by the Queen and all at Court for her gay and happy nature, and married in 1500 to Guy Comte de Laval, Seigneur de la Roche, a young and handsome knight deeply attached to his estates in Brittany.

Her mother, a niece of Louis XI.'s wife, had been brought up at the French Court. She died when Charlotte was quite a child, and the widowed husband, Frederick III. of Naples, being, through his political misfortune, unable to care properly for his little daughter, sent her, at the age of ten, to the Court of Charles VIII. where she was graciously received by the King, and as early as 1496 established as one of the Queen's maids of honour under the title of the Princesse de Tarente, with a salary of 300 Tours pounds. She had her own suite of attendants, including a governess, nurse, several young ladies, an esquire, a chaplain, two valets-de-chambre, and two grooms. She had a litter for her own use, a mule and several horses, in fact she was treated with all the respect due to royal princesses. Anne was especially fond of her, and after Charles VIII.'s death, when she left Paris for her Duchy, a sad and tender farewell took place between them, the Queen giving Charlotte a toilet service of massive silver. When Cæsar Borgia visited France in 1498, bringing with him a Cardinal's Hat for Georges d'Amboise and, as we have already seen, the Bull for the dissolution of the marriage of Louis XII. and Jeanne de France, he was at once smitten with the charm and beauty of Charlotte d'Aragon, wore her colours and device, and determined not only to obtain her father's consent to a marriage, but to possess himself of the principality of Tarento. Brantôme gives a long account of the splendid procession which accompanied him, and of the luxury displayed by Borgia during this visit. The fifty gentlemen who followed him were robed in velvet, silk, and cloth of gold; Borgia himself, mounted on a large horse, caparisoned with cloth of gold set with pearls and other precious stones, was clad in a parti-coloured dress of red satin and cloth of gold, glittering with priceless jewels. His cap was decorated with a double row of large rubies of wondrous lustre, and round his neck he wore a collar worth 30,000 ducats.

The thought of so powerful and vicious a son-in-law filled Frederick with horror, not only for his daughter's sake but for his own, for he feared, not unreasonably, to be deprived of a kingdom which he held with no certain hand. Cæsar was not easily to be appeased when his desires were thwarted. As soon as the dissolution of Louis' marriage was completely assured, he begged him to persuade Frederick to consent to his union with the Princess. Directly Charlotte herself knew of Borgia's designs, she repudiated the idea as perfectly impossible, and nothing could conquer her repugnance. Cæsar demanded a definite reply, and Charlotte bravely gave it him. Sure of the support of her father and of the new Queen, her mistress, and knowing that Louis would not be displeased, she refused absolutely to have anything whatever to do with such an atrocious man, saying she would never marry the son of a priest, and a fratricide—infamous not only because of his birth but still more so because of his own actions. It required no small courage to defy so unscrupulous and powerful a man, and the Queen highly praised her favourite's conduct.

In compensation for the care she took in procuring suitable alliances for these girls, Anne expected them blindly to submit to her will in all things. She would not allow the slightest deviation from the rules which she had established, and would not pardon the errors which even a lawful love might lead them to. A daughter of the House of Rohan and a niece of the Maréchal de Gié had bitter experience of this; the matter made a great stir at Court, and Marguerite d'Angoulême made it the subject for one of her stories in the *Heptameron*. Anne's mother was Marie of Brittany, the sister of Duke Francis II., and she was therefore first cousin to the Queen. Her offence was falling in love with an

illegitimate son of the House of Bourbon
and meeting him alone in the chapel of the
Castle. In the *Heptameron* we may read
of the Queen's anger and the reproaches
with which she overwhelmed the poor girl.
"Rolandine," as Marguerite calls her, knew
well that Anne had never really cared for her,
because Jean de Rohan, her father, had
served France for many years to the detriment
of Brittany. With a calm and almost joyous
face she said that she had known for a long
time that the Queen did not like her, and that
her hatred for the father was visited on his
child. But for that she would have been
married long ago like so many others, and she
had resolved to become a nun just before
meeting her lover. It was very unjust that
the Queen should treat her as "méchante," for
between the Bastard and herself there had been
no intimacies except the promise of marriage,
the exchange of a ring and a kiss; she had
hoped God might grant her wish that her father
should give his consent to the match. "I
have neither offended God nor my conscience,"
she said, "for I waited till I was thirty to see

what you and my father would do for me, preserving my youth in such chastity that no one can reproach me with anything. Becoming an old maid without the hope of finding a match suitable to my rank, I resolved to marry someone of my own choice, not to give pleasure to the eyes, forsooth, for you know that he is not handsome, nor through pride or ambition, since he is poor and of little position, but as a reward for the sincere love he bears me, for the great virtues with which he is endowed, and for which everyone agrees in praising him."

"Rolandine" had other talks with the Queen, which, far from appeasing, annoyed her the more. Anne accused her of obstinacy and hardness of heart: "If the King and your father will believe me," she said, "you will be put in a place where you will sing a different tune." "Madame," replied Rolandine, "you are my mistress and the greatest Princess in Christendom, and for nothing in the world would I fail in the respect I owe you, but I protest that I have only done what honour suggested and what God would approve. Since I am forsaken by all, I have a Father in

Heaven to whom I commit my cause; He will sustain me I am sure." It was impossible to shake " Rolandine's" courage.

The Bastard vainly tried to soften Louis' heart, but he had been prejudiced against the unhappy pair by his wife. One day he went to the King and told the whole story. The King, after listening to him, said, " Do you mean to tell me that you have married her?" " Yes, Sire, but in promises only; if it be your good pleasure, however, there shall be a fulfilment of them."

But the King gave no reply, and with bowed head returned to the Castle. Soon afterwards an order was given to arrest the Bastard, but, warned in time, he fled and reached the frontier. As for " Rolandine," shut up in her own room for some time, she refused to listen to the proposals made for an alleviation of her lot if she would break the engagement she had made. She was therefore sent away to her father, who confined her in a castle in the midst of a forest, where she remained several years. In 1508, Mercurin de Gatinara, the ambassador of Margaret of Austria at the

A Twice Crowned Queen

Court of France, was ordered by his mistress to speak to the Queen in favour of " Rolandine's " betrothed, the Bastard of Liège. He received the following reply : "The girl was no longer with her, and her father kept her in such close confinement that it was not in her power to give her up to 'ung tel galant,' it was also not known whether she was alive or dead, but there were rumours that she was dead."

Anne de Rohan was not dead. After a long captivity she heard that her Bastard had taken refuge in Germany, and that he had married another woman. She then implored and obtained her father's forgiveness, and in her fortieth year, 1517, married her cousin, Pierre de Rohan, Seigneur de Fontenoy, the third son of the Maréchal de Gié.

Although Anne allowed implacable hatred to carry her to extremes of injustice, which must have grieved Louis as much in this case as in that of the Maréchal de Gié, she showed generally great care and generous solicitude, not only for her maids of honour, but also for all members of her own and her husband's households. All, whatever their birth or rank, went to her with their needs, and were seldom refused assistance. She constantly gave presents in addition to the ordinary and generous salary which everyone received. She liked the members of her household to be suitably dressed, and often gave them extra money to buy velvet, satin, or woollen material. If they were ill she took care they should want for nothing, gave pensions to those who had grown old in her service, and if they lost relations through death, she defrayed the expenses of the funeral, or gave the survivors mourning garments.

As a rule, when the Queen's anger was past she repented and forgave the offence though not without some difficulty, and, moreover, she was not blind to the violence of her character, for she used to beg her confessor not to grant her absolution until she had made reparation for the injury and harm her anger had caused to others. In spite of all the services Louis de la Trémouille had rendered to Charles VIII. and Louis XII., Anne could never forget that it was he who had gained the victory of Saint-Aubin-le-Cormier over her father, Duke Francis II. Louis' conduct was far otherwise. Taken prisoner by La Trémouille at the same battle, he granted him full and complete pardon when he became King, and entrusted the command of his army to him. He many times tried to persuade his "Bretonne" to be equally generous, but a whole year passed before he succeeded. At last, on the 11th of April 1500, the King, who was in Dauphiné, received the news that Lodovico Sforza had been taken prisoner, and that La Trémouille, by his military skill, had just put an end to the war. The Queen was at Lyons, so Louis hastened back, and joyously entering her room, exclaimed laughingly, "What do you think, Madame, La Trémouille has just taken Lodovico Sforza!" Anne replied that she was glad, but that she could not forget another victory he had gained over her own father. Louis replied, "I assure you that no King of France has ever had so loyal a servant, nor one more fortunate in all his undertakings; I shall reward him in such a manner that other captains will be proud to serve me." The Queen was silent, but from this day she looked favourably on La

Trémouille, and when opportunity offered, did not hesitate to extol his virtues.

Anne also gave much attention to the pages and children of noble birth attached to her suite; they were all dressed alike in a handsome livery of the Queen's own colours—yellow, red, and black before the death of Charles VIII., red and black afterwards. She gave them presents on the Feast of the Holy Innocents, on New Year's Day, and at Easter, but always on condition that they had been to confession. She exacted from these children the same obedience and good conduct as from all others who served her, and the slightest fault was punished severely. Brantôme's father, François de Bourdeille, was for eight years the Queen's head page, and always rode on the first mule of her litter, M. d'Estrées leading the back mule; if one of these mules went too fast and forced the other to follow its lead, the litter was shaken and the Queen, inconvenienced on these occasions, would cry out: "Bourdeille, you and your companion will be whipped, I assure you!" It was no good throwing the excuse of this unequal pace one upon the other, for the Queen would accept no excuses, and had them both flogged well and soundly.

In the autumn of 1493, Ferrando, a youth of sixteen, arrived at the French Court. He was the second brother of "la prima donna del mondo," Isabella d'Este, and great were the preparations that he should be equipped in a manner befitting a son of the Duke of Ferrara. The number of attendants of all kinds was carefully fixed; forty-six horses and mules were brought with him, as well as two horses named "Reale" and "Roseghino," the latter especially good for exercise in the tilt-yard, which his father had given him. Duke Ercole, who was then on a visit to his son-in-law Lodovico il Moro at Milan, writes thus to the boy's mother, Leonora:

"As to the clothes for Don Ferrando to wear, it is not necessary that he should take many ready made, because every day the fashion changes in France; but let him be given some silk stuffs to be made up when he has got there. I would remind your Ladyship that we have information that the French in their attire use black velvets, as also black silks and damask, and that they hardly use any other silk, excepting that now and then one sees there a jerkin of fine crimson silk."

He adds particulars concerning the equipment of Ferrando's escort, and the four gentlemen who were "continually to eat with our son, because such is the custom in France, and it will be an honourable thing." Leonora, alas! was too ill to attend personally to the provisions for her son's departure, and it must have been a great grief for such a loving mother to part from her boy. She died soon afterwards on October 11th, before Ercole, her husband, could reach Ferrara. Ferrando himself hurried back, but was too late even to be present at his mother's funeral, and at once departed again for France, where the King and Queen gave him a sympathetic and gracious reception. Duke Ercole kept up a constant correspondence with his son; and hearing that it would be well to present some "cose odorifere" to the King and Queen, but finding himself too badly provided with such things to be able to make such a present to their Royal Majesties as would be worthy of them and him, he sends him, by the Count Baldiserra da Montecucculo, "three grains of musk, two small which are set as you will see, and one large one which is not otherwise set. We are sending them to you in order that you may be able to make presents with them on your own account, showing that you have had something from home. Those two little ones you can give, if you think fit, to two of those principal great ladies, one, for instance, to the Duchesse de Bourbon and the other to the Duchesse d'Orleans, and that bigger one you could give from yourself to that most serene Queen, without giving it in our name. We have not thought well to have it set, because we do not quite know the way they have over there of setting such things. And so, likewise, you could give to His Majesty two horns of civet, which we are sending you by the said Count Baldiserra, in the way that we have told you." A little later the Duke wrote to reprove his son for giving himself too much to ease, and not using fitting diligence "in following and serving the Majesty of that most Christian King." He tells Ferrando that he was sent to France to make himself good for something, and urges him to throw all his soul into the service of the King. "We know that you have plenty of talent, and that you know what your duty is, and that, if you wish, you can do yourself credit." *

Luxury and comfort in itself she did not care for, her antiquated and rather middle-class Breton home did not give her tastes in that direction, but all the same she surrounded herself with the so-called luxury of the age, feeling it was incumbent on her as Queen to do so. Comfort, as we understand it, did not then exist in the French Court, for chairs were only provided for the King and Queen, princesses and ladies of noble birth were allowed cushions on the floor to sit upon, but other ladies of lower rank had to stand, sometimes for hours at a time. Beds, however, were sumptuous and richly decorated, and were sometimes given as presents, as we have already seen when François d'Angoulême presented his bride with a handsome bedstead. Anne always took a travelling bed supplied with straps and locks

* Edmund G. Gardner, M.A., *Dukes and Poets in Ferrara.*

with her on her various journeys, and a large leather bag for cutlery, salt-cellars, etc., another for bread and provisions, and a third was fitted with flagons for wine and water. Great precaution was needful in those days with regard to the food for the royal table, and their wine was always kept in a specially padlocked cabinet.

The Queen's chests, in which her linen, ribbons, head-dresses were kept, were full of sachets filled with powder made from Provence roses, musk, or violets. In 1492, Jean Georget, the Queen's merchant in stuffs, supplied her apothecary with red silk to make scent sachets "for the said lady."

The Queen made frequent use of baths, and as a special room was not in those days set apart for the purpose, they used large vats in the shape of troughs, with covers, heated by iron caldrons standing on tripods underneath.

Louis XII. and his wife spent much money in laying out and embellishing the gardens at Blois; there was an upper and a lower garden, the last and smaller of the two being known as the "Jardin de la Reine." Not only was Anne very fond of plants and flowers, but also of animals, birds and dogs especially, of which she possessed several kinds. Among her dogs were nine large greyhounds, sent for from Lower Brittany where the breed was famous. These dogs wore collars of black velvet, ornamented with gold ermines. In her own room she had a sweetly singing linnet, and on one occasion a man named Louis des Sauvages, from Languedoc, brought her many little foreign birds clever at catching flies on the wing, to amuse her.

She loved to hear the songs of Brittany, and kept four Breton minstrels in her service. The following event in her life shows how fond she was of music and singing. This is how an inhabitant of Chartres relates the story concerning the big bell of the cathedral. "There are four bells which always ring in harmony . . . one of them is called Anne of Brittany because it was given by the Duchess. . . . She came to Chartres in 1510, and, delighted with the singing of a choir-boy called Le Fève, she begged the clergy to let her have the child, and when thanking them said, 'You have given me a little voice, but I will give you a big one!'"

A Twice Crowned Queen

This bell was also called " La Cloche des Biens,"
because this same Le Fève, to whom the
Queen subsequently gave a canonry at Chartres,
presented the sum of 3000 livres to the clergy,
provided they should ring this bell from the
Sunday after Easter to Trinity Sunday for one
hour a day.

Jugglers and actors were often admitted to
the Castle to perform before the Queen. In
March 1492, François de Nicole of Florence
received thirty-five Tours pounds to maintain
his niece Lucrezia, whom he had brought to
dance before the Queen. The Queen of
Sicily's fiddlers and others who came from
Paris to amuse Anne and her ladies were also
generously rewarded.

Her shrewd and subtle mind knew in a
marvellous way how to read the secret intentions of those admitted to her presence on
important matters, and Louis after giving
audience to ambassadors frequently sent them
to the Queen that she might have an opportunity of exercising this gift. It was the duty
of M. de Grignaux, the first Chamberlain, to
introduce them. He was one of the most

polished men at Court, and knew several languages. Anne learned from him words in Spanish, Italian or German which she would mingle in her speech to those who visited her. Grignaux was of a facetious and merry nature like the King, and Brantôme tells us that one day when the Queen asked him for a fine speech in Spanish which she might address to the Archduke's ambassador, who was arriving on the next day, he, in a fit of merriment, laughingly told her "quelque petite falauderie," to use Brantôme's expression, which she learned with the greatest care. The next day, when the time for the audience was approaching, M. de Grignaux told all to the King, who laughed much about it, but hastened to his "Bretonne" to warn her against uttering words which should not be spoken by any modest woman! Anne, however, did not relish the joke at all; she burst into such a rage, in spite of the King's good humour, that nothing would content her until Grignaux was banished from her sight. Louis pacified the Queen by saying that the chivalrous Grignaux would not have failed to warn her in time; so, yielding to his entreaties, she at length consented to pardon and receive him again at Court.

During King Louis' many absences in Italy, Anne found consolation in the midst of her ladies and poets. She encouraged, though in rather a haphazard way, men whose knowledge and wit might shed lustre upon their country and their patroness, for at this time art, science, and letters flourished only in the palaces of kings and nobles. Jean Marot, father of the poet Clément Marot, took the title of "poète de la magnanime Anne de Bretagne," and was never weary of extolling the Queen's virtues and generosity; in 1512, after her serious illness, he wrote a poem to celebrate her convalescence. Poetry itself, in those days, rarely lost its character of fulsome adulation and servility. Anne patronised a competition on a subject for which she had a special affection, the exaltation of the female sex. She herself was at the head of contemporary ladies by her virtues, wit, and strength of mind, and she wished her sex to share in society the position of respect and esteem which she herself had acquired at Court, and she deeply resented the injustice of men with regard to women. She ordered her poets, therefore, to avenge the female sex, and—the signal given —attacks began against all satirical books composed in hatred or scorn of women. Jean de Meung had, it was said, been whipped by the ladies of the Court of Philippe le Bel because of his audacious and insulting epigrams against the feminine sex! The orators, inspired by Anne of Brittany, tried to stifle the mocking laugh of such discourteous adversaries by a concert of praises in the admired manner of the day, Anne being firmly convinced that men could not stand a comparison with women. A Breton poet, named Disarvoez Penguern, composed a "Genealogy of Anne of Brittany" in a long and monotonous rhyme, meant no doubt to be chanted to a slow and plaintive air by the "fileuses" of old Armorica.

History was patronised as much as poetry, and Anne did not spare money in the interest of historical compilations which should con-tribute to the honour of her reign, and specially favoured those which extolled her Duchy.

Anne, surrounded by her ladies in a State

room, would often receive a book from its author, or one of the poets would ask for an audience to recite a piece of verse in the form of a panegyric on some subject chosen by the Queen the day before at table. The rest of the day was devoted to "Hours" and meals, the evening to needlework, when one of the secretaries would read romances, history, legends of saints, or poetry, or learned men would discourse and dispute with all the resources of their intellect. The education of princes thus went on all their lives; and if the verses composed in their honour were full of flattery, graver discourses with instruction were often inculcated by the paid orators.

The custom of having a buffoon or fool in the house was more common in this reign than in any other; every lord, clerk, or layman had an ugly or deformed fool, dressed in his master's livery, with a cap with ass's ears and a bauble, and these grotesque creatures, hideous to look upon and sad to hear, were intended to afford amusement like monkeys or parrots. Wise fools were out of fashion. There were two in the King's household, Caillette and Triboulet. Triboulet was Louis' favourite, and went with him on all his journeys; his chief talent consisted in contradicting everyone; but he sang, danced, and talked so pleasantly that no one was angry.

Anne of Brittany's library consisted of manu-scripts and printed works in Latin, Italian, Greek, and Hebrew, as well as in French. Over one thousand volumes taken from Naples were given by Charles VIII. to his Queen, and by her added to the collection she had brought from the Castle of Nantes after her marriage. Her library, therefore, must have contained from thirteen to fifteen hundred volumes; and doubt-less works on religion, science, philology, and history were more numerous than profane works, such as the "fabliaux" or romances of chivalry. She was particularly liberal to printers and founders of libraries, and many important works were dedicated to her. All the manuscripts which she ordered to be composed, transcribed, and illuminated have unfortunately not been preserved, but the few which have, bear witness to the care, skill, and knowledge of those to whom she committed the work.

Some account must here be given of Anne's celebrated *Book of Hours* which is preserved in the Louvre. It is not only one of the most perfect specimens of French art at the end of the fifteenth century, but a witness to the delicate taste of the Queen. The plants, flowers, and fruits of Touraine, that sunny garden of France, decorate its pages, and we think of Anne's love for the works of Nature, and the gardens she laid out at Amboise and Blois. Her own portrait and those of the saints of her country are reproduced several times. The volume is composed of two hundred and forty leaves of fine white vellum, enriched with numerous paintings, initial letters, vignettes, and designs of flowers, fruit, and insects. The paintings decorating the calendar represent the occupations of the country for the month. The landscapes are charming, and give a very good idea of the varied, fresh, and sunny nature of the country on the banks of the Loire which the artist probably had before his eyes. The illumination for the month of April is worthy

A Twice Crowned Queen

of special attention, because the Castle of Blois may easily be recognised. At the foot of the page is one of the gardens which the Queen specially loved, and which bore her name. In this garden a young woman, dressed as Anne usually was, sits on the grass twining a wreath, another on her knees before her offers the seated figure a basket full of different flowers. The artist has no doubt depicted the Queen in her garden at Blois, charming away her leisure moments with the flowers she loved. It is said that the flowers and plants painted on the margins of this beautiful book were all to be found in the Castle gardens. The Latin name of each plant is inscribed in purple letters at the top of the page, and the common French name in letters of gold on a foundation of colour at the foot.

Among the forty-nine full-page illustrations, is one representing Anne kneeling before a prie-Dieu on which lies open a Book of Hours. She is clad in the costume she wore on ordinary occasions, and wears the Breton cap. Behind her stand her three patron saints, St. Ursula, St. Margaret, and St. Anne, who places her left hand on the Queen's shoulder, and with her right seems to be drawing her attention to the crucified Jesus on the opposite page. Another depicts St. Catherine dressed as a queen in one of the beautiful costumes Anne used to wear on State occasions. Experts have traced four different hands in the execution of this lovely volume, and doubtless the work was in progress for many years. The first page bears the date 1499, the year of her marriage with Louis, but the portrait of herself must certainly have been painted when she was nearly thirty.

Anne honoured and encouraged artists of all kinds, and from the royal accounts we may judge of the number and importance of artistic works carried out by her orders. Among the jewels is one by Jean Barbedor of Paris, given by the Queen to her first husband in 1492. On this day she also gave presents to her tapestry workers, to show her appreciation of the work they had executed for the Castle of Amboise. In October 1494 the Duke and Duchess of Bourbon paid a visit to the King,

and the two large courts of the Castle were
hung with these tapestries in their honour.
Among the various subjects depicted on them
was the battle of Formigny, gained by Charles
VII. in 1450, and in which the English were
defeated.

Charles VIII. brought many artists back with
him from Naples, sculptors, painters, illumina-
tors, workers in gold, wood-carvers, tailors,
embroiderers, and gardeners. These were
established at Tours, and summoned by the
King and Queen when required at the Castle.
In 1496 one of them was employed by Anne
to paint on white leather, decorations for her
bed.

One of the greatest sculptors of the Renaissance, Michel Colomb, born at St. Pol de Léon
about 1460, was commissioned by Anne in
1507 to carve the beautiful tomb, now in
Nantes Cathedral, to the memory of her father
and mother. Another celebrated sculptor of
Tours was Jean Just, who wrought the tomb
of Louis XII. and Anne of Brittany at Saint
Denis.

The Queen formed a large collection of

religious pictures, mounted in gold, silver, ivory, or wood. Many were brought from Italy by Charles, and were doubtless painted by the great Italian masters of the fifteenth century; unfortunately, however, the inventory of the Castle gives no details of these. There were also portraits of illustrious persons, among which were those of Lodovico Sforza and his son Philip.

The gold and silver plate was designed and wrought by skilled workers in the precious metals, and embroidered stuffs in gold and silk and jewels of all kinds are noted in the inventory. Anne, as we have before said, was generous with her riches, and whatever the rank or quality of the persons admitted to her presence, each carried away a present as a souvenir of the visit, as Brantôme relates in *Dames Illustres*. Another writer of the seventeenth century, who had not seen the then unpublished memoirs of the Sieur de Bourdeille, speaks thus of the magnificence of her gifts : " It is well known that this most generous Princess had a cabinet full of diamonds, pearls, rubies, emeralds, and other precious stones, of which she gave presents to the wives of captains and heroes who had gained honour and glory in war, and to those who had faithfully served King Louis XII., her husband, who was not so lavish himself, because he feared thereby to offend his poor people, of whom he was the "Father."

Anne spent much of her wealth in building ships to guard her coasts against the depredations of the English, and among the most famous of these was a huge man-of-war called *Marie la Cordelière*, which survived an expedition against the Turks in 1501, and was twice visited by the Queen-Duchess at Brest. Ten years afterwards, *La Cordelière* was attacked off the island of Ushant by the English flag-ship *The Regent*, and a deadly fight ensued. The two vessels grappling together became a veritable field of carnage, in which many thousands of men disputed the victory. The captain of *La Cordelière*, Hervé Portzmoguet, a Breton of heroic soul, seeing that he would have to give in, did not hesitate to fire his ship with those he was fighting, and soon afterwards *Marie la Cor-*

A Twice Crowned Queen

delière and *The Regent* disappeared together. Those on board perished in the midst of the flames, or were swallowed up by the sea.

Anne had no love for England, and in 1512, De La Motte was constantly passing to and fro between France and Scotland, urging James IV. to war with England for the sake of the ancient league. Louis XII. naturalised all Scots then resident in France, and it may be of interest to know that the torquoise ring, found on James' finger after the fatal battle of Flodden, is said to be the same which Anne of Brittany sent him in May 1512, when she dubbed him her knight, and begged him for her sake to strike a blow on the English crown.*

Thus closes my short account of the twice crowned Queen of France, and I can only hope that the interest it has given me to collect details of her romantic life may be shared by those who care to devote any spare time to the perusal of this little history.

* Andrew Lang's, *History of Scotland.*

Printed by MORRISON AND GIBB LIMITED, *Edinburgh*

A CATALOGUE OF
BOOKS PUBLISHED
BY EVELEIGH NASH
LONDON, AT 32 BED-
FORD STREET, W.C.

SEPTEMBER 1906

NEW AND FORTHCOMING BOOKS.

GENERAL LITERATURE.

FAMOUS BEAUTIES OF TWO REIGNS.
Charles II.—George III.   By MARY CRAVEN.   Photogravure
Portraits.   Demy 8vo, 21s. net.   [*September.*]

THE CHATEAUX OF TOURAINE.
By MARIA HORNOR LANSDALE.   Pictures by JULES GUERIN.
Royal 8vo, cloth gilt, gilt top, 24s. net.   [*September.*]

THE NEW RUSSIA.
By LIONEL DECLE.   Demy 8vo, 7s. 6d.   [*Ready.*]

THE GREAT LORD BURGHLEY (WILLIAM CECIL).
By MARTIN HUME, Author of "The Wives of Henry VIII.," etc.
Photogravure Portrait.   Demy 8vo, 12s. 6d.   [*Ready.*]

IN THE DAYS OF THE DANDIES.
By ALEXANDER, LORD LAMINGTON.   Introduction by Sir HERBERT
MAXWELL, Bart.   Portraits.   Crown 8vo, 3s. 6d. net.   [*Ready.*]

A TWICE CROWNED QUEEN, ANNE OF BRITTANY.
By CONSTANCE, COUNTESS DE LA WARR.   With Portraits.   Demy
8vo, 7s. 6d. net.   [*September.*]

A ROYAL TRAGEDY.

By Chedomille Mijatovitch, Late Envoy Extraordinary and Minister Plenipotentiary of the King of Servia to the Court of St. James. Demy 8vo, 7s. 6d. *[September.]*

NOOKS AND CORNERS OF OLD ENGLAND.

By Allan Fea. Demy 8vo, 10s. 6d. *[October.]*

SUCCESS AMONG MEN.

By Dr. Emil Reich. Crown 8vo, 6s. *[October.]*

FICTION.

THE INVASION OF 1910,

With a Full Account of the Siege of London. By William Le Queux. Naval Chapters by H. W. Wilson. Introduction by Lord Roberts. Crown 8vo, 6s. *[Ready.]*

THE POWER OF THE PAST.

By Daniel Lesueur. Crown 8vo, 6s. *[September.]*

THE MATRIMONIAL LOTTERY.

By Charlotte O'Conor Eccles. Crown 8vo, 6s. *[September.]*

THE MANAGER'S BOX.

By John Randal. Crown 8vo, 6s. *[October.]*

THE SURGE OF WAR.

By Norman Innes. Crown 8vo, 6s. *[October.]*

GOD'S OUTPOST.

By Cullen Gouldsbury. Crown 8vo, 6s. *[October.]*

STORIES ABOUT WOMEN AND THE WEST.

By CHARLES MARRIOTT.   Crown 8vo, 6s.   [*October.*]

LAWFUL ISSUE.

By JAMES BLYTH.   Crown 8vo, 6s.   [*October.*]

THE PARADISE OF THE WILD APPLE.

By RICHARD LE GALLIENNE, Author of "The Quest of the Golden Girl," etc.   [*In preparation.*]

A DRAMA IN SUNSHINE.

By HORACE A. VACHELL.   Crown 8vo, 6s.   [*October.*]

THE GREY DOMINO.

By Mrs. PHILIP CHAMPION DE CRESPIGNY, Author of "The Rose Brocade."   Crown 8vo, 6s.   [*Ready.*]

SONS OF THE MILESIANS.

By the COUNTESS OF CROMARTIE, Author of "The Web of the Past."   Crown 8vo, 6s.   [*Ready.*]

THE HOUSE IN SPRING GARDENS.

By Major ARTHUR GRIFFITHS, Author of "The Passenger from Calais," "The Rome Express," etc.   Crown 8vo, 6s.   [*Ready.*]

RAFFLES,

The Amateur Cracksman.   By E. W. HORNUNG.   Crown 8vo, 6s.   [*Ready.*]

WHISPERS ABOUT WOMEN.

By LEONARD MERRICK.   Crown 8vo, 6s.   [*Ready.*]

4

GENERAL LITERATURE.

TEN TUDOR STATESMEN.

By ARTHUR D. INNES, Author of "England under the Tudors." Portraits. Demy 8vo, 15s. net.

WITH THE EMPRESS DOWAGER OF CHINA.

By KATHARINE CARL. Illustrated. Demy 8vo, 10s. 6d. net.

VERSAILLES AND THE COURT UNDER LOUIS XIV.

By JAMES E. FARMER. With Seventy Illustrations. Demy 8vo, 15s. net.

Recollections of the Court of William IV. and the early Court of Queen Victoria.

MY MEMORIES.

By the COUNTESS OF MUNSTER. Portraits. Demy 8vo, 12s. 6d.

"To turn over the leaves of this book is like opening the lid of an old china tea-pot fragrant with pot-pourri made in the days of our grandmothers, the sweet scent of which fills us with dream-memories of old forgotten things. The quaintly stiff etiquette of old English Court life, the glimpses of old-world characters whose oddities belong to the past, the anecdotes of great personages, the very memory of whom is now fast fading away ; the reminiscences of exciting incidents in European history which we now read without a tingling of pulse, the description of manners and customs which have disappeared completely in the turmoil of modernity, are flavoured with that old-fashioned charm which we find in Fanny Burney's 'Evelina' or Mrs. Gaskell's 'Cranford.'"—*Daily Chronicle.*

2   5

WORKS BY MARTIN HUME.

THE WIVES OF HENRY VIII.

AND THE PARTS THEY PLAYED IN HISTORY. By
MARTIN HUME, "Author of the Courtships of Queen Elizabeth,"
"The Love Affairs of Mary Queen of Scots," etc. With Portraits.
Demy 8vo, 18s. net.

"A handsome volume, which will be a permanent possession to any one who
is wise enough to purchase it."—*Pall Mall Gazette.*
"The most deeply interesting book Major Hume has written."—
Athenæum.

THE COURTSHIPS OF QUEEN ELIZA-BETH.

By MARTIN HUME, Author of "The Love Affairs of Mary Queen of
Scots." Revised Edition, with New Chapters on the Personal
Relations between Elizabeth and her Favourites. Demy 8vo, 12s. 6d.

"We would counsel a perusal of this very remarkable volume, which, besides
being in the highest degree entertaining, furnishes utterly new views of the
spacious times of the great Elizabeth."—*Daily Telegraph.*

Uniform with the above Work.

THE LOVE AFFAIRS OF MARY QUEEN OF SCOTS.

By MARTIN HUME. With Portraits. Demy 8vo, 12s. 6d.

"This distinguished historian approaches as near to being severely judicial
as any historian is ever likely to be."—*Standard.*

SPANISH INFLUENCE ON ENGLISH LITERATURE.

By MARTIN HUME, Examiner in Spanish in the University of London.
Demy 8vo, 7s. 6d.

"A sound and thoroughly exhaustive study of a fascinating subject."—
Daily Telegraph.
"A fascinating book."—*Morning Post.*

WORKS ON RUSSIA.

Important Work on Russian Influence in the Orient.

ASIATIC RUSSIA.

By GEORGE FREDERICK WRIGHT, LL.D., F.G.S.A. With Maps and Illustrations. Two Volumes. Royal 8vo, 32s.

"A book which may with great advantage be consulted on almost every Russian question."—*Athenæum.*

"For many years will hold the field as a text-book."—*Daily Chronicle.*

WITH THE RUSSIANS IN PEACE AND WAR.

Recollections of a Military Attaché. By Colonel the Hon. F. A. WELLESLEY, former British Military Attaché in Russia. With Six Photogravure Portraits. Demy 8vo, 12s. 6d.

"Should be read by all who wish to understand the tremendous catastrophe which is developing under our eyes in 1905."—*Daily Telegraph.*

Uniform Works by Carl Joubert.

RUSSIA AS IT REALLY IS.

By CARL JOUBERT. Demy 8vo, 7s. 6d.

"Mr. Joubert has lived nine years in the Russian Empire. He has visited every government of it, and associated with every class. . . . With such an equipment one expects a book of no uncertain tone. This is precisely what Mr. Joubert gives us."—*Westminster Gazette.*

THE TRUTH ABOUT THE TSAR AND THE PRESENT STATE OF RUSSIA.

By CARL JOUBERT. Demy 8vo, 7s. 6d.

"Full of interesting and even sensational disclosures.—*Daily Telegraph.*

"This book, on the other hand, fascinates because it paints terrible contingencies of the near future."—*Standard.*

THE FALL OF TSARDOM.

By CARL JOUBERT. Demy 8vo, 7s. 6d.

"'The Fall of Tsardom' is a book to be read."—*Spectator.*

7

AN EYE-WITNESS IN MANCHURIA.

By LORD BROOKE, Reuter's Special Correspondent in Manchuria. Demy 8vo, 7s. 6d.

"Stands out as a model of what the work of a war correspondent should be."—*Times.*

THE SIEGE AND FALL OF PORT ARTHUR.

By W. RICHMOND SMITH, Special Correspondent with the Japanese Army besieging Port Arthur. Preface by Lieut.-General Sir W. G. NICHOLSON, K.C.B. Maps and Illustrations. Demy 8vo, 12s. 6d. net.

"The most important book which the Far Eastern War has yet produced."—*Manchester Guardian.*

WITH THE COSSACKS.

Being the Story of an Irishman who rode with the Cossacks throughout the Russo-Japanese War. By FRANCIS M'CULLAGH. Illustrated. Demy 8vo, 7s. 6d. net.

THOUGHTS FROM MONTAIGNE.

Selected by CONSTANCE, COUNTESS DE LA WARR. With an Introduction and a Biographical Study. Foreword by EGERTON CASTLE. Pott 8vo, 2s. 6d. net.

LIVES OF THE QUEENS OF ENGLAND.

By AGNES STRICKLAND. In Sixteen Volumes. Demy 8vo, Twelve Guineas net the set.

N.B.—A new Edition in Sixteen Volumes, profusely illustrated with collotype, coloured, and hand-coloured Illustrations.

THE PRIVATE LIFE OF TWO EMPERORS.

William II. of Germany and Francis Joseph of Austria. Second Edition. Two Volumes. Ten Illustrations. 24s. net.

"The facts are all clear and authentic."—*Westminster Gazette.*
"These volumes are undeniably well informed."—*Pall Mall Gazette.*

8

SECRET HISTORY OF THE COURT OF ENGLAND

From the Accession of George III. to the Death of George IV. By LADY ANNE HAMILTON. Two Vols. Illust. Demy 8vo, 30s. net.

THE LIFE OF SIR HENRY VANE THE YOUNGER.

By WILLIAM W. IRELAND. Fully Illust. Demy 8vo, 12s. 6d. net.
"A work of notable interest and worth."—*Scotsman.*

THE LOVE AFFAIRS OF GREAT MUSICIANS.

By RUPERT HUGHES. With numerous Illustrations. Two Volumes. Crown 8vo, 10s. net.

ASPECTS OF BALZAC.

By W. H. HELM, Author of "Studies in Style," etc. Crown 8vo, buckram, 3s. 6d. net.

THREE BEAUTIFUL GIFT-BOOKS.

in Ornamental Binding.

MILTON'S ENGLAND.

By L. A. MEAD. With Illustrations. 6s. net.

Uniform with "Milton's England."

DICKENS' LONDON.

By FRANCIS MILTOUN. With Illustrations. 6s. net.

Uniform with "Dickens' London."

A WOMAN'S WALKS.

By LADY COLIN CAMPBELL. With Water-Colour Portrait. 6s. net.

THE COMING REACTION.

A Brief Survey and Criticism of the Vices of our Economic System. By LEGISLATOR. 320 pages. Demy 8vo, 7s. 6d.

"Whoever 'Legislator' may be, there can be no disputing the fact that he has given the world the most trenchant and original criticism yet produced of the doctrines and theories on which free trade is based."—*Daily Mail.*

"The strongest plea for the abandonment of England's free trade policy which has yet been made."—*New York Sun.*

"Many books have been written against Socialism, but few popular writers have subjected it to so destructive a criticism as 'Legislator.'"—*Sunday Times.*

THE FISCAL DISPUTE MADE EASY.

By W. H. MALLOCK, Author of "The New Republic." Crown 8vo, 1s.

AN ABSENT-MINDED WAR.

By A BRITISH OFFICER. Fourteenth Edition. 192 pages. Crown 8vo, cloth, 2s. 6d. ; paper, 1s.

". . . It should be read by every citizen who wishes to know his duty."—*Daily Mail.*

"Every word of this little shilling volume is worth weighing and quoting, and it would be well if the Army League or some really patriotic organisation could place a copy in the hands of every elector in the country and compel him to read it, and heckle the candidate for his vote and interest upon it afterward."—*Pall Mall Gazette.*

A COMMON-SENSE ARMY.

By the AUTHOR of "An Absent-Minded War." Fourth Edition. 190 pages. Crown 8vo, cloth, 2s. 6d. ; paper, 1s.

"This little book abounds in sound principles and excellent common sense."—*Times.*

"Whichever way we take them, his pages contain much suggestive and instructive reading."—*Westminster Gazette.*

A Charming Gift=Book.

LETTERS TO A DÉBUTANTE.

By LADY JEPHSON. Small crown 8vo, gilt top, 3s. 6d.

" Bright, chatty, and smartly written."—*Daily Telegraph.*

FICTION.

SIX SHILLING NOVELS.

THE BLUE PETER.

By MORLEY ROBERTS, Author of "The Promotion of the Admiral,"
"Captain Balaam of 'The Cormorant,'" etc.

THE LAPSE OF VIVIEN EADY.

By CHARLES MARRIOTT, Author of "The Column," "Mrs. Alemere's
Elopement," etc.

BARDELYS THE MAGNIFICENT.

By R. SABATINI, Author of "The Tavern Knights."

HE LOVED BUT ONE.

The Story of Lord Byron and Mary Chaworth. By F. FRANKFORT
MOORE, Author of "The Jessamy Bride," etc.

" A great deal of loving study has gone to the making of this fine story."—
World.

THE PARSON'S WOOD.

By VIOLET A. SIMPSON, Author of "The Bonnet Conspirators," etc.

" Here is a capital story . . . which holds the reader until the end is
reached."—*Pall Mall Gazette.*

CAPTAIN MAROON.

A Romance. By ROBERT STUART.

" Real, vivid, and thrilling."—*Pall Mall Gazette.*

DEBORAH'S LIFE.

By JAMES BLYTH, Author of "Celibate Sarah," etc.

"Deborah is a variant of Tess, and she certainly holds the attention."—*Pall Mall Gazette.*

THE THIRD KISS.

By HERBERT FLOWERDEW, Author of "A Celibate's Wife," etc.

"The humour is of a particularly fine type."—*Pall Mall Gazette.*
"An exceedingly clever story."—*Scotsman.*

THE FLIGHT OF GEORGIANA.

By R. N. STEPHENS, Author of "A Gentleman Player," etc.

"A capital tale, told in an easy, natural style, of 18th century manners—not in town but the country—the inn, the hall, and the road."—*Times.*

THE WIND-JAMMERS.

By T. JENKINS HAINS.

"Mr. Hains knows a ship, and can tell a story; and has an adequate sense of the dramatic possibilities of sea life."—*Daily Mail.*

THE MATRIMONIAL BUREAU.

By CAROLYN WELLS.

"Acute in its observation of character . . . an amusing and enjoyable story."—*Scotsman.*

THE WEB OF THE PAST.

By the COUNTESS OF CROMARTIE, Author of "The End of the Song."

"Admirers of Celtic glamour will assuredly add this volume to their shelves."—*Daily Mail.*

THE PROCESSION OF LIFE.

By HORACE ANNESLEY VACHELL, Author of "Brothers," "The Hill," etc.

"Mr. Vachell's book is one to get and to read, and, when read, to keep for reading again."—*Daily Telegraph.*

OUTCASTS OF THE EAST.

By FLORENCE BAILEY.

" This powerful book is sure to be widely read."—*Scotsman.*

" It is, in a word, a novel worth reading—and thinking over."—*Daily Telegraph.*

BROTHERS OF PERIL.

By THEODORE ROBERTS.

" The story never flags, and is admirably written."—*Manchester Courier.*

THE SEVEN STREAMS.

By WARWICK DEEPING, Author of " Uther and Igraine," " Love among the Ruins."

" ' The Seven Streams ' is a fine tale . . . full of strong emotions . . . picturesque description is Mr. Deeping's special gift, and he has it in large measure."—*Morning Post.*

THE NUNNERY WALL.

By ELIZABETH HOLLAND (Lady Owen).

" This romance ranks at all events among the finest first books of all the novelists."—*Yorkshire Post.*

" Of absorbing interest."—*Pall Mall Gazette.*

MRS. ALEMERE'S ELOPEMENT.

By CHARLES MARRIOTT, Author of " The Column."

" We welcome the new book."—*Times.*

" Clever and powerfully written."—*Daily Telegraph.*

" An outstanding novel . . . a work of art."—*Daily Chronicle.*

" By far the best book Mr. Marriott has yet written."—*Daily Mail.*

THE PASSENGER FROM CALAIS.

By Major ARTHUR GRIFFITHS, Author of " The Rome Express," etc.

" A plot as involved as it is thrilling."—*Pall Mall Gazette.*

" It is not every author who can write stirring fiction like this."—*Daily Express.*

MEN OF THE NORTH SEA.

By WALTER WOOD.

"A more acceptable volume of stories . . . was never published . . . These simple men, with their confiding trust in every printed word, and their amusing ignorance, are heroes when the time comes, and their little-known life is well worth the faithful, telling representation here given with such timeliness and force."—*Pall Mall Gazette*.

THE GOLDEN THREAD.

By TOM GALLON, Author of "Tatterley," etc.

"The best that Mr. Gallon has produced for some time."—*Morning Post*.

"A very pretty, amusing, and uncommon story."—*Daily Chronicle*.

"Wholesome and pleasant."—*Standard*.

THE OTHER WORLD.

By F. FRANKFORT MOORE, Author of "The Jessamy Bride," etc.

"It is the sort of volume that proves an excellent companion—together with a deck chair and an idle hour."—*Scotsman*.

HIGH NOON.

By ALICE BROWN, Author of "The Mannerings," etc.

"She has ideas and rouses thought ; in these matters of love she has a high spiritual standard which will appeal to all but the out-and-out rationalists, and even they may find that her intelligent 'tossing' of a tangled question lets in some light and air."—*Times*.

"No one could read this new volume . . . without recognising that here is a woman of genius, with a fine romantic spirit free from that note of vulgarity and self-assertion that is so marked in so much of the fiction produced to-day."—*Sphere*.

A MAID AT LARGE.

By A. LEAF, Author of "Strawberry Leaves."

A DAUGHTER OF KINGS.

By KATHARINE TYNAN, Author of "A Red Red Rose," etc.

"A charming Irish novel."—*Morning Post*.

The Romance of a Maid of Honour in the days of King George I.

THE ROSE BROCADE.

By Mrs. PHILIP CHAMPION DE CRESPIGNY, Author of "The Mischief of a Glove."

"A book which will most deservedly find many delighted readers."—*Bookman.*

SOPHY BUNCE.

By THOMAS COBB, Author of "Mrs. Belfort's Stratagem."

"Singularly pleasant, and told with great skill."—*St. James's Gazette.*

A Great Human Story.

SETH OF THE CROSS.

By ALPHONSE COURLANDER, Author of "The Taskmaster."

"A powerful story."—*Morning Post.*
"'Seth of the Cross' is a good book that should have a popular, as well as an artistic success."—*Pall Mall Gazette.*

THE BRIGHT FACE OF DANGER.

By R. N. STEPHENS, Author of "An Enemy to the King," "A Gentleman Player," etc.

"'The Bright Face of Danger' is a good tale of adventure drawn from an interesting period of French history. The plot is an ingenious one, and there is no lack of excitement."—*Westminster Gazette.*

JEZEBEL'S HUSBAND.

By MARK ASHTON, Author of "She Stands Alone."

"This is a story of the city of Damascus, 3000 years ago. It is a fine piece of work, in which the reader's interest is never allowed to flag."—*Outlook.*

MRS. BELFORT'S STRATAGEM.

By Thomas Cobb, Author of "The Intriguers," "A Change of Face," etc.

"A bright, clean example of the English novel. . . . An excellently told, bright, and well-written story."—*Morning Post.*

THE AFTER COST.

By K. M. Edge, Author of "Ahana," etc.

"One quality the writer has, which must always rank high in a novelist's equipment. She has the instinct for story, and that, after all, is one of the essentials."—*Athenæum.*

THE GREEN EYE OF GOONA.

By Arthur Morrison, Author of "The Red Triangle," "Tales of Mean Streets," etc.

"A capital piece of work."—*Standard.*

THE TRIUMPH OF MRS. ST. GEORGE.

By Percy White, Author of "Park Lane," "The West End."

"In none of the novels that have gone to make his reputation as a satirist of certain phases of West-End life is the dialogue more sparkling or the character-drawing more vivacious."—*Athenæum.*

"Now mordantly amusing, now poignantly sad."—*Vanity Fair.*

RACHEL MARR.

By Morley Roberts.

"Mr. Morley Roberts's finest achievement."—*Morning Post.*

"Beautifully conceived."—*Academy.*

"A fine novel. It raises its author to a high place."—*Vanity Fair.*

"One of the most remarkable novels of the generation."—*Queen.*

THE LAND OF SILENCE.

By G. B. Burgin, Author of "The Way Out," "The Shutters of Silence."

"It has the indefinite charm of all tales told by the born story-teller."—*Times.*

THE ADMIRABLE TINKER.

By EDGAR JEPSON.

. The Admirable Tinker is the greatest boy hero since Huckleberry Finn and Tom Sawyer.

" Mr. Jepson has a light touch, and his gaiety is infectious."—*Star.*

THE WINE OF LOVE.

By H. A. HINKSON, Author of "O'Grady of Trinity."

"Sparkling with Irish wit and humour, this novel is perhaps the best that has yet appeared from the author's pen."—*Outlook.*

THE LETTERS WHICH NEVER REACHED HIM.

ANONYMOUS.

" Surely the most pathetic love-letters that ever were written."—*Outlook.*

LORD AND LADY ASTON.

By E. H. COOPER, Author of " Mr. Blake of Newmarket," etc.

" Mr. Cooper's book is worth pondering, for if one half of its grim indictment rests on fact, what are we to think of the huge racing carnival which will occupy Society from now till the end of the season."—*British Weekly.*

HIS EMINENCE.

By LADY HELEN FORBES, Author of "An Outcast Emperor," etc.

" Full of dramatic episodes, which hold the reader's interest until the last page."—*Daily Telegraph.*

THE STRONGER CLAIM.

By ALICE PERRIN, Author of " East of Suez."

" Cannot fail to attract all who feel the fascination of the gorgeous East."—*Pall Mall Gazette.*

" Strongly felt and conceived."—*Times.*

TRENT'S TRUST.

By BRET HARTE.

"We find in it the touch of a vanished hand. . . . One would be sorry to miss the book."—*Athenæum.*

THE DIARY OF A YEAR.

By Mrs. CHARLES H. E. BROOKFIELD.

"Mrs. Brookfield avoids monotony because she writes well. She knows the world, and her touch, though it is light, is very sure."—*Punch.*

A RED RED ROSE.

By KATHARINE TYNAN.

"A wholesome and pleasant story."—*Glasgow Herald.*

THE INTRIGUERS.

By THOMAS COBB.

"Always an agreeable and entertaining writer, 'The Intriguers' is quite his best book so far."—*Daily Mail.*

THE MANNERINGS.

By ALICE BROWN.

"A strong, subtle, and sympathetic work."—*St. James's Gazette.*

THE MYSTERY OF MURRAY DAVEN- PORT.

By R. N. STEPHENS.

"To the jaded novel-reader its perfect newness will be a most genuine refresher."—*Pall Mall Gazette.*

STRAWBERRY LEAVES.

By A. LEAF.

" A very able book. The people in its pages are real human beings, so real that one cannot help thinking that they must be taken from life."—*Queen*.

THE NEVER-NEVER LAND.

By WILSON BARRETT, Author of " The Sign of the Cross."

"There is a sustained movement about it that keeps the reader constantly interested."—*Glasgow Herald*.

THE COUNTESS AND THE KING'S DIARY.

By PERCY WHITE.

" Mr. Percy White's work is both ingenious and amusing."—*St. James's Gazette*.

NOBODY'S BABY.

By TOM GALLON.

" A very pathetic idea is embodied in this charming story, and it furnishes a convenient plot on which to hang a subsidiary romance."—*Spectator*.

THE PRIME MINISTER AND MRS. GRANTHAM.

By CARLTON DAWE.

" The author has a faculty of shrewd observation and a dramatic talent that have turned out between them a very interesting story."—*Vanity Fair*.

A MAN-AT-ARMS.

By CLINTON SCOLLARD.

" The story is distinctly a success."—*Spectator*.

19

THE RED TRIANGLE.

By ARTHUR MORRISON.

"A book which is sure to attract many readers."—*Observer*.

ONE PRETTY PILGRIM'S PROGRESS.

By FLORENCE BRIGHT, Author of "The Vision Splendid."

"The interest of the story is always sustained and carries the reader along with it."—*Morning Post*.

THE CRUCIBLE.

By A. F. SLADE, Author of "A Wayside Weed," etc.

"The book is brightly and interestingly written."—*Daily Mail*.

THE WRONG ROAD.

By Major ARTHUR GRIFFITHS.

THE PASSION FOR ROMANCE.

By EDGAR JEPSON, Author of "The Admirable Tinker."

"The hero is treated from a refreshingly new standpoint. He is a new sort of hero as well as a fresh specimen in individuals : neither villain, saint, nor martyr, but simply a possible human being with some strong characteristics."—*Athenæum*.

SAINT PORTH.

The Wooing of Dolly Pentreath. By J. HENRY HARRIS.

"A Cornish tale of remarkable picturesqueness, although natural and touching, full of quaint pictures of a marvellously decorative people."—*Saturday Review*.

THREE SHILLINGS AND SIXPENCE.

A Large New Edition in cloth of the late
Mr. Wilson Barrett's Great Novel.

THE SIGN OF THE CROSS.

By WILSON BARRETT.

THE PROMOTION OF THE ADMIRAL.

By MORLEY ROBERTS.

"Very delightful as well as very unusual."—*Spectator.*

CAPTAIN BALAAM OF "THE COR-MORANT."

By MORLEY ROBERTS, Author of "The Promotion of the Admiral,"
etc.

"A book full of smiles."—*Daily Telegraph.*

A SET OF FLATS.

By Major ARTHUR GRIFFITHS.

"A detective story of the best kind. . . . There will be a general desire on
the part of the public for more work of the same nature from the same
author."—*Daily Express.*

THE PASSING OF ARTHUR.

By COSMO HAMILTON.

"An amusing farrago of personalities, impudences, and absurdities."—
Vanity Fair.

"A cleverly sustained 'squib' which will be chuckled over by readers of
every shade of political opinion."—*World.*

THE BLUE FOX.

By W. H. HELM.

"We can promise for the enlightened reader far more entertainment in
'The Blue Fox' than he will find in the more insistently humorous novels of
the day."—*Times.*

TWO SHILLINGS AND SIXPENCE.

THE ROME EXPRESS.

By Major ARTHUR GRIFFITHS.

"Any reader who opens this book with the resolution that he will read a chapter of it and then resume his ordinary occupations is likely to be surprised speedily out of such good intentions. The story grips you like a vice."—*Sketch*.

A SEA COMEDY.

By MORLEY ROBERTS, Author of "A Son of Empire," "The Western Avernus," etc. 2s. 6d.

"'A Sea Comedy' is great fun, and the only fault we have to find with it is that it is too short."—*Athenæum*.

CLARE MONRO.

The Story of a Mother and Daughter. By HANNAH LYNCH. 2s. 6d.

"There are passages in this brief story for which no praise could be too high. . . . The book well answers to the description of the series which 'is designed to meet the taste of readers who desire a swiftly-moving, well-written, dramatic tale of moderate length, with continuity and action from the first page to the last.' Such readers will have their desires gratified, though the movement is more of thought than incident, and it results from a breach of the Seventh Commandment."—*Sheffield Daily Telegraph*.

SONGS AND SONNETS.

By OSWALD NORMAN. 5s.

"A delicate and reflective mind informs the whole volume, and whether Mr. Norman writes of the everlasting verities, or . . . whether he touches upon the vanities of human life, his lines have always an uplifting quality, which should assure the poet the lasting goodwill and devotion of many readers."—*Referee*.

INDEX TO AUTHORS.

EVELEIGH NASH.

Hume, Martin. Courtships of Queen Elizabeth.

Hume, Martin. Love Affairs of Mary, Queen of Scots.

Hume, Martin. Spanish Influence on English Literature.

Hume, Martin. The Great Lord Burghley (William Cecil).

Innes, Arthur D. Ten Tudor Statesmen.
Innes, Norman. The Surge of War.
Ireland, William W. Life of Sir Henry Vane the Younger.

Jephson, Lady. Letters to a Débutante.
Jepson, Edgar. Admirable Tinker.
Jepson, Edgar. Passion for Romance.
Joubert, Carl. Russia as it Really Is.
Joubert, Carl. Truth about Tsar.
Joubert, Carl. Fall of Tsardom.

Lamington, Lord. In the Days of the Dandies.

Lansdale, Maria Hornor. The Chateaux of Touraine.

Leaf, A. Maid at Large.
Leaf, A. Strawberry Leaves.
Le Gallienne, Richard. Paradise of the Wild Apple.

Legislator. Coming Reaction.
Le Queux, William. The Invasion of 1910.

Lesueur, Daniel. The Power of the Past.
Lynch, Hannah. Clare Monro.

M'Cullagh, Francis. With the Cossacks.

Mallock, W. H. Fiscal Dispute Made Easy.

Marriott, Charles. Lapse of Vivien Eady.

Marriott, Charles. Mrs. Alemere's Elopement.

Marriott, Charles. Stories about Women and the West.

Mead, L. A. Milton's England.
Merrick, Leonard. Whispers about Women.

Mijatovitch, Chedomille. A Royal Tragedy.

Miltoun, Francis. Dickens' London.

Moore, F. Frankfort. He Loved but One.
Moore, F. Frankfort. Other World.
Morrison, Arthur. Green Eye of Goona.
Morrison, Arthur. Red Triangle.
Munster, Countess of. My Memories.

Norman, Oswald. Songs and Sonnets.

Perrin, Alice. Stronger Claim.

Randal, John. The Manager's Box.
Reich, Dr. Emil. Success Among Men.
Roberts, Morley. Captain Balaam of "The Cormorant."
Roberts, Morley. The Blue Peter.
Roberts, Morley. Promotion of the Admiral.
Roberts, Morley. Rachel Marr.
Roberts, Morley. Sea Comedy.
Roberts, Theodore. Brothers of Peril.

Sabatini, R. Bardelys the Magnificent.
Scollard, Clinton. Man-at-Arms.
Simpson, Violet A. Parson's Wood.
Slade, A. F. Crucible.
Smith, W. Richmond. Siege and Fall of Port Arthur.
Stephens, R. N. Bright Face of Danger.
Stephens, R. N. Flight of Georgiana.
Stephens, R. N. Mystery of Murray Davenport.
Strickland, Agnes. Lives of the Queens of England. (16 vols.)
Stuart, Robert. Captain Maroon.

Tynan, Katharine. Daughter of Kings.
Tynan, Katharine. Red Red Rose.

Vachell, Horace Annesley. Procession of Life.
Vachell, Horace Annesley. A Drama in Sunshine.

Wellesley, Col. the Hon. F. A. With the Russians in Peace and War.
Wells, Carolyn. Matrimonial Bureau.
White, Percy. Countess and the King's Diary.
White, Percy. Triumph of Mrs. St. George.
Wood, Walter. Men of the North Sea.
Wright, George Frederick. Asiatic Russia. (2 vols.)

24